bird can sing

Rick Burnett Baker

bird can sing

ISBN-13: 978-1537704128

ISBN-10: 1537704125

Printed in the U.S.A.

Bootstrap Publishing
mkd@bootstrappublishing.net

This book is dedicated to
Ina Jean Stovall Garner, whose
creations of art and photography
have encouraged and inspired me
throughout my life, and to

Betty Jo Stovall Baker, who
imparted her artistic and musical talents
to me from an early age, and who
continues to be a guide and
loving mother to this day.

Acknowledgments

My sincere thanks and gratitude go to the following people, without whom this project may never have seen the light of day.

Pat Zarpentine, who has been instrumental in changing my mindset with her three little words: Quality Of Life.

Damien Duong for decades of friendship and being my devil's advocate, helping me to question my directions, and keep a balanced perspective.

Mark Stechschulte for always offering positive feedback and encouragement.

Eddie Tang, a superb artist and friend from my days in Singapore, who constantly encourages me to question the traditions of how we think about personal satisfaction and notions of success.

Vincent Chye, a designer extraordinaire, and long-time friend from Singapore and Thailand, for constantly encouraging me to "just be the artist."

Michelle Flechette Ames, for her on-going website technical support.

To artists, writers, and fellow bloggers Steven Leak, Cheryl Cato, Vicki Lane, Tess Kincaid, Julian Hakim, Nyl Frederick Lim, Karl Lester M. Yap, and Lo Lee Ta, who have encouraged and helped me in my writing endeavors through the better part of the last eight years.

And my thanks and gratitude to all my co-workers and friends on social media who have, and continue to offer their support and encouragement. And for listening to my rants on a daily basis!

I *view my artwork through the lens of everyday conversations, observations, and emotional responses to my surroundings. Photo poetry, for me, helps make sense of what I see or feel, and allows me to express a "local" worldview that I sometimes have difficulty expressing in simple words.*

Art and poetry surround us. In our everyday lives of the mundane, many of us don't take the time to actually think about our surroundings and how they may reflect our personal, as well as collective, lives. What, for example, does graffiti tell us aside from the common, visceral thought that it is simply vandalism? What is that subtle intellectual prodding I sense when watching a sunset? What are, and are there, absolute truths in human endeavor?

My intent is to first express what I sense as the deeper meaning to these images in relation to my personal beliefs or philosophies.

My hope is that my efforts will encourage others to take the extra few seconds each moment, day or week to reflect more quietly, thoughtfully, or viscerally about their surroundings and emotions.

Reflection, after all, is also poetry and art.

~ Rick Burnett Baker

bird can sing

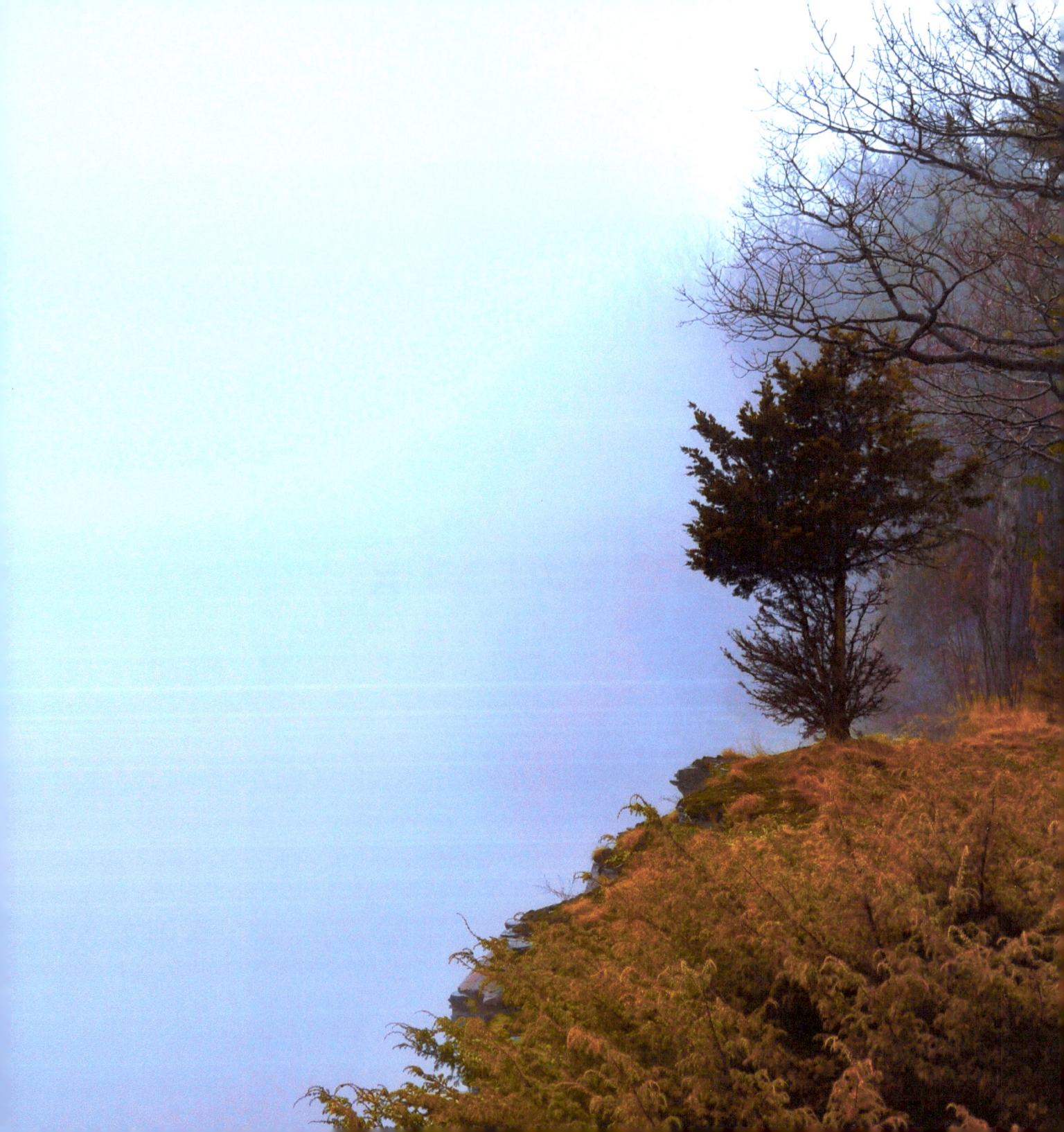

I was frightened of the forest
until I saw the void.

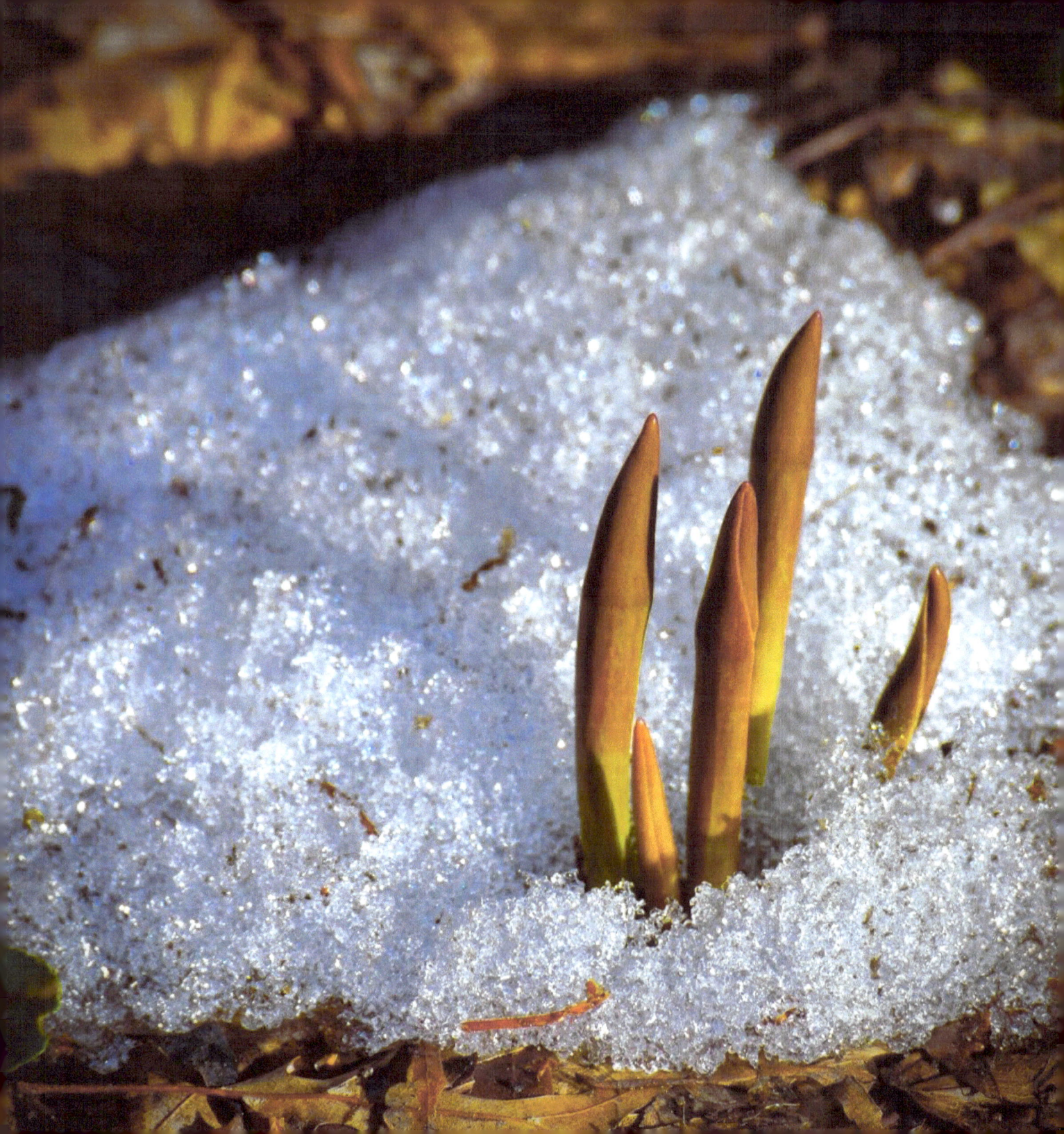

If you believe in the
power of humans,

a quiet walk through the woods on
a cold spring day will show you
what power really is.

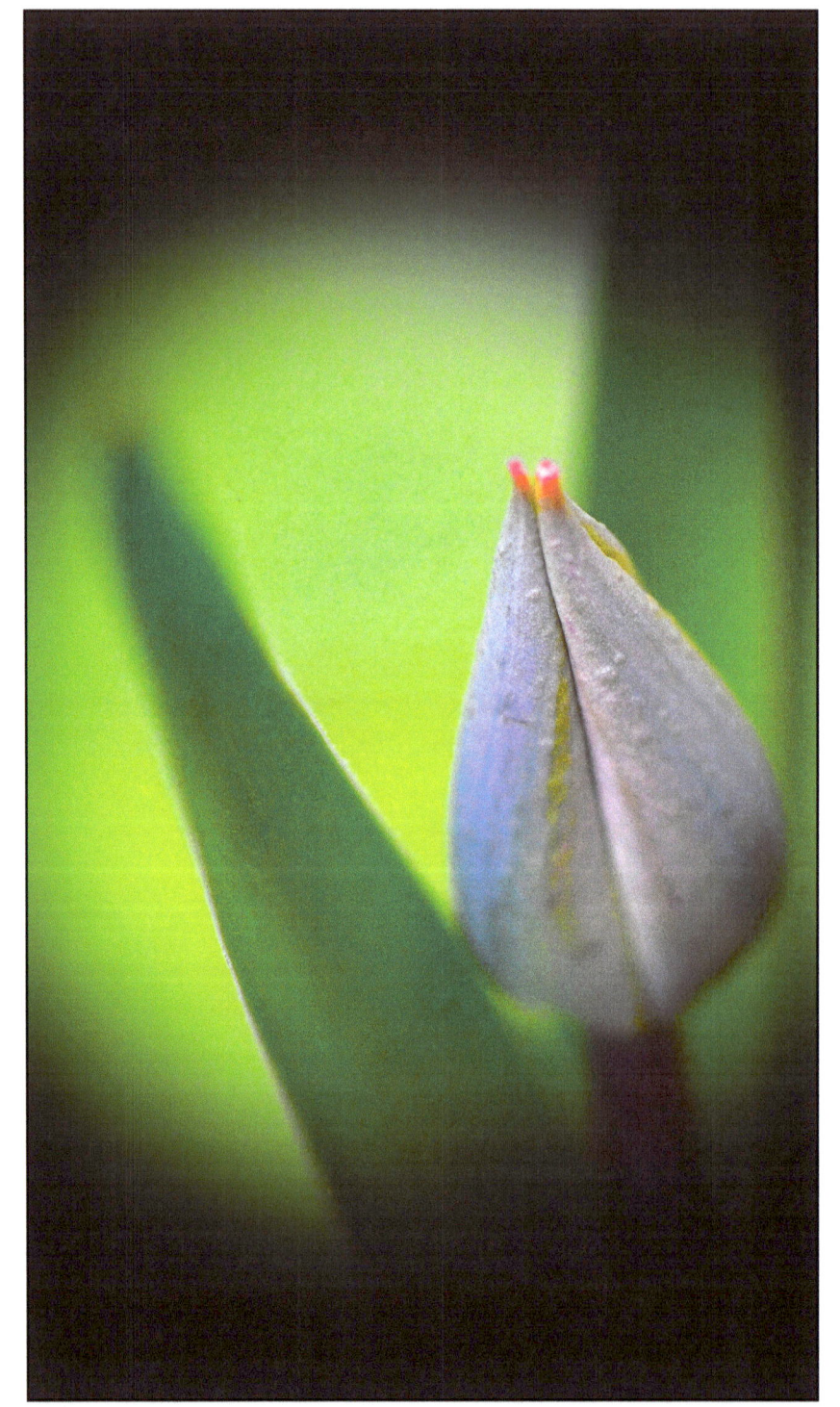

There is
birth today,
when flesh
meets sky,
where all is
promised,
and all else
forgiven.

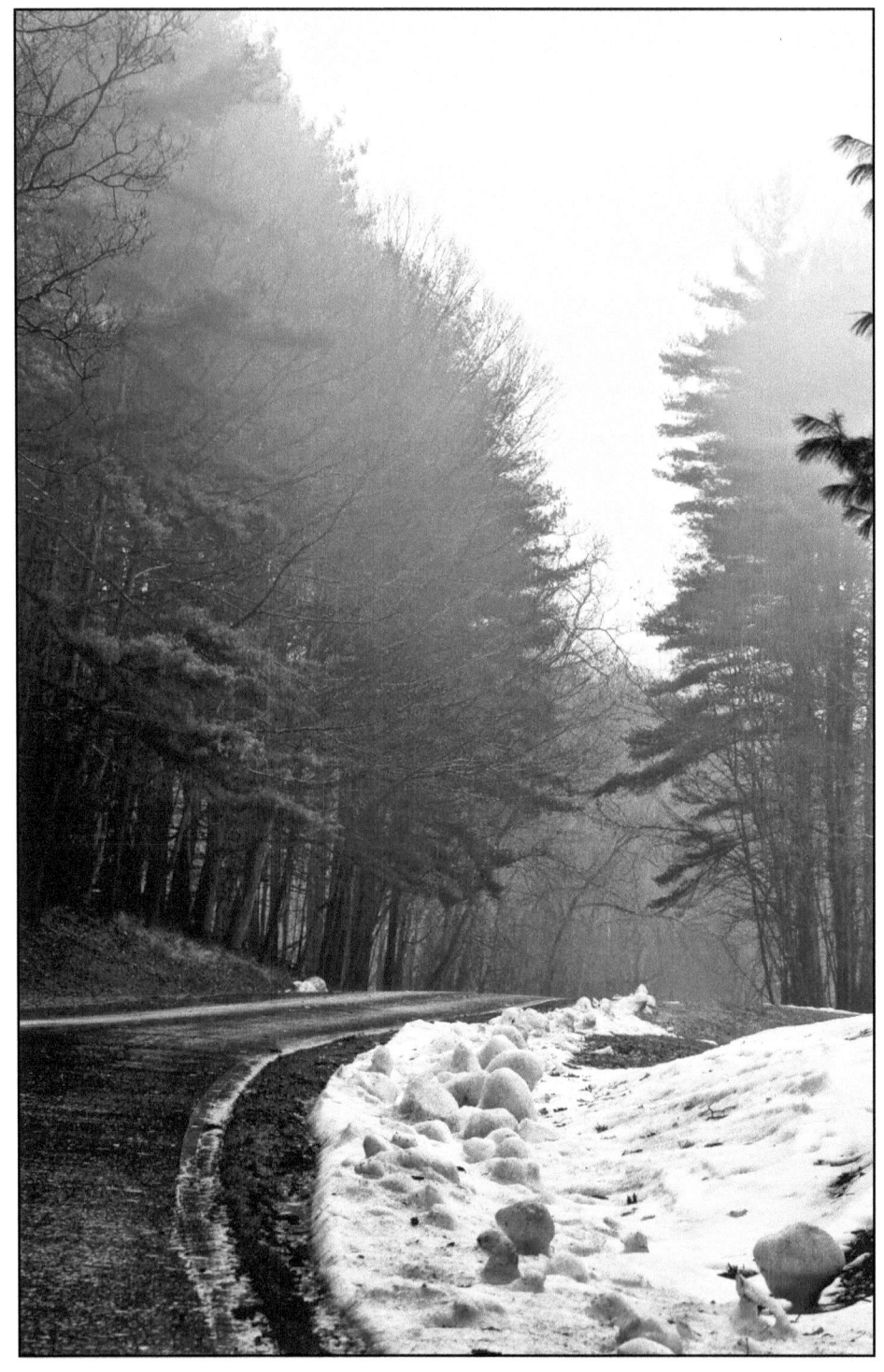

Defy

Nature's order is defiance.
Due course vilifies and
verifies as seasons spar.

I'm captive to seasonal toil,
violent beauty of winter.
Spring renews, and I, too, am restless.

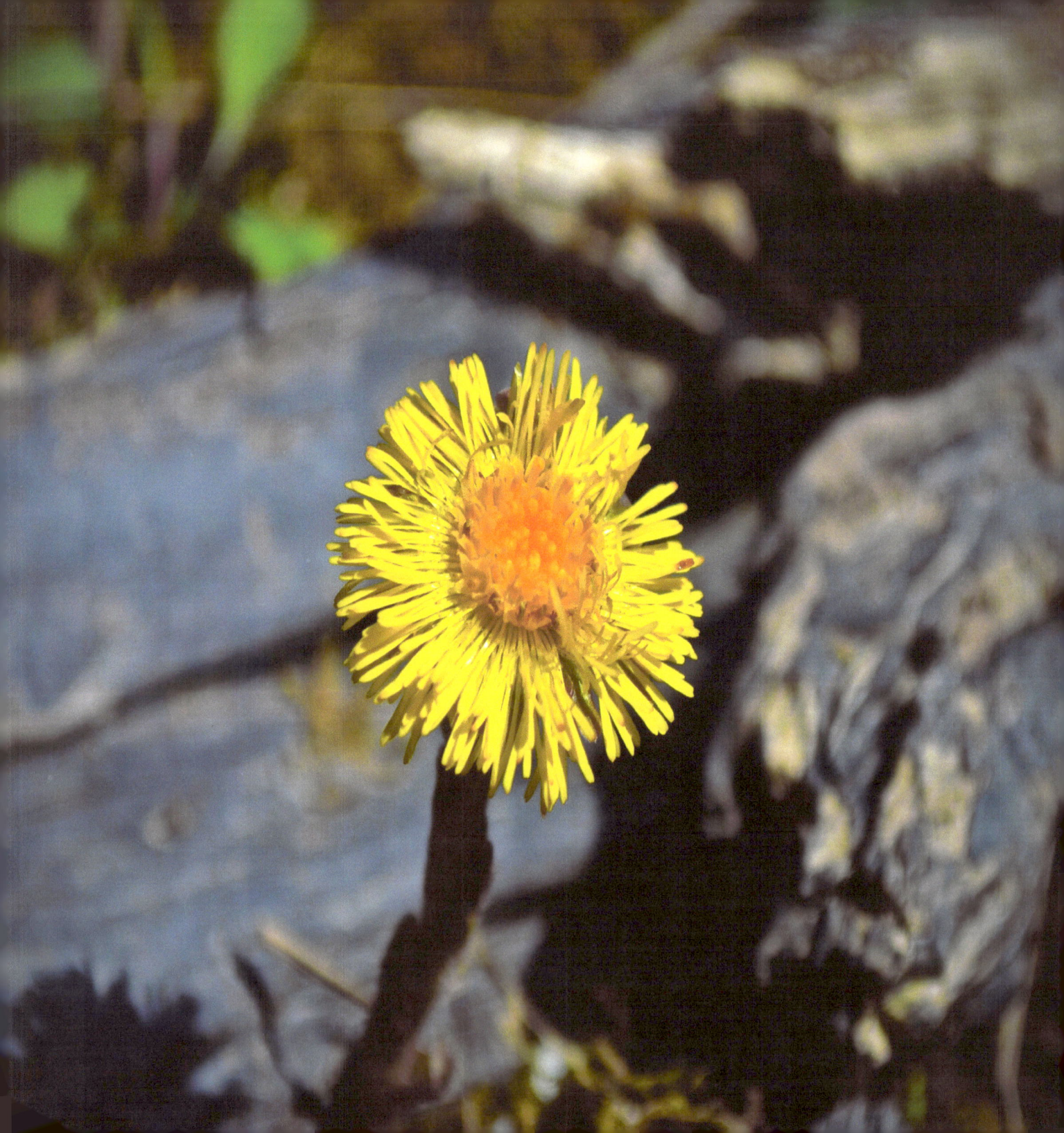

Spontaneity creates itself.

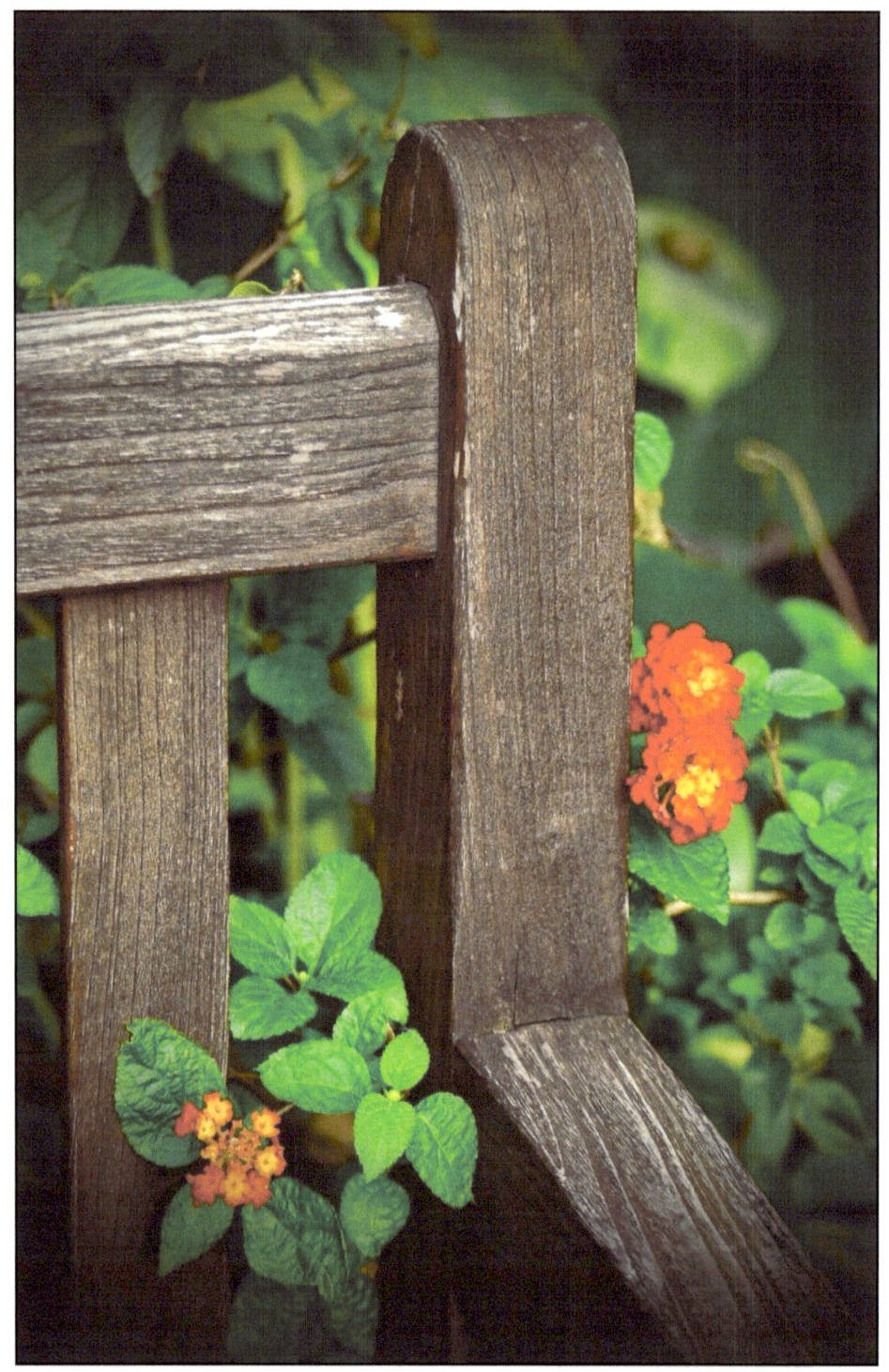

What is strength
if not delicate?

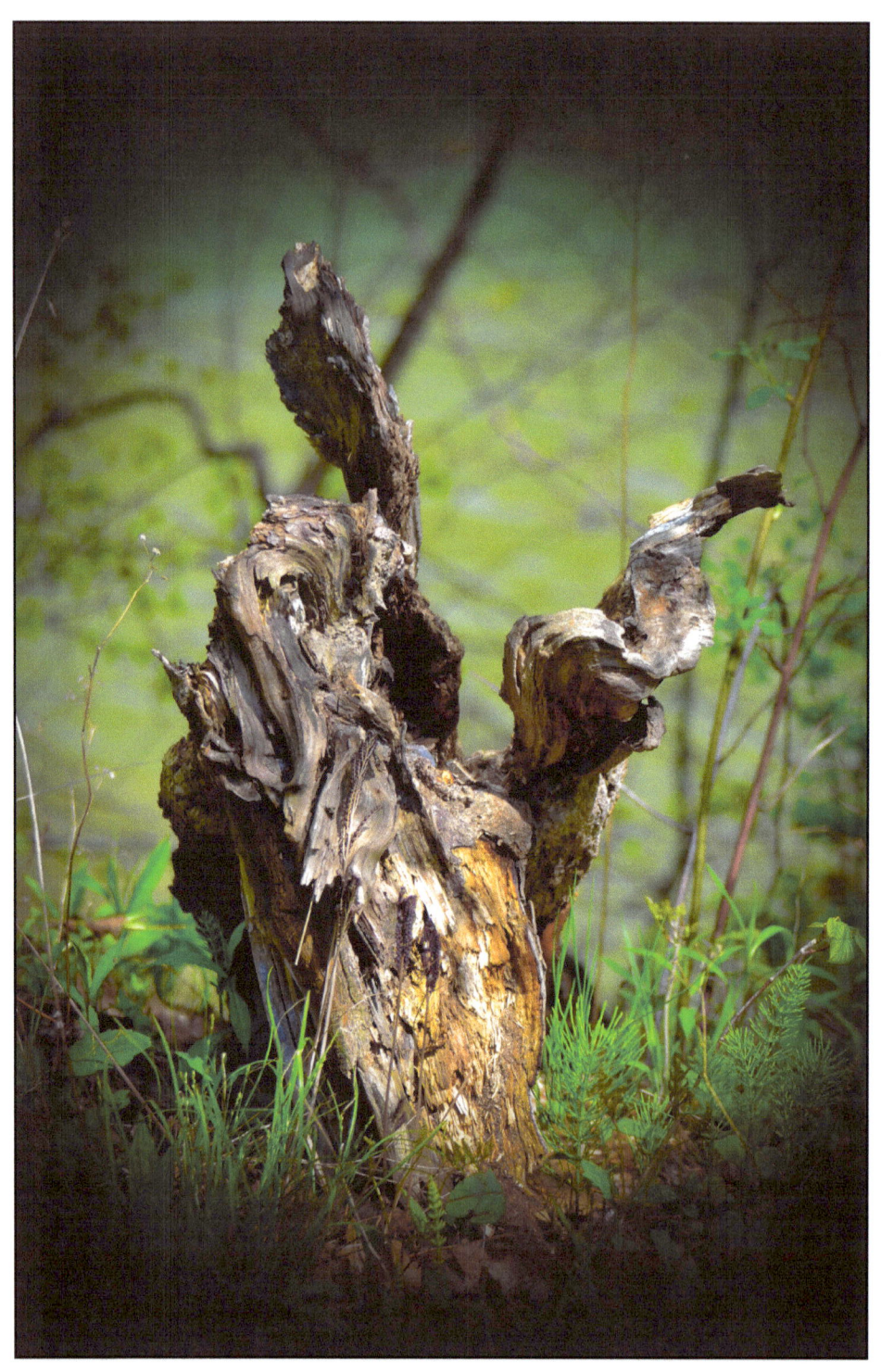

Exile

You, me, the others are
silent universes waiting
for creation to begin again.

Let's sit here in the meadow
and watch the past: It holds
no future that isn't now.

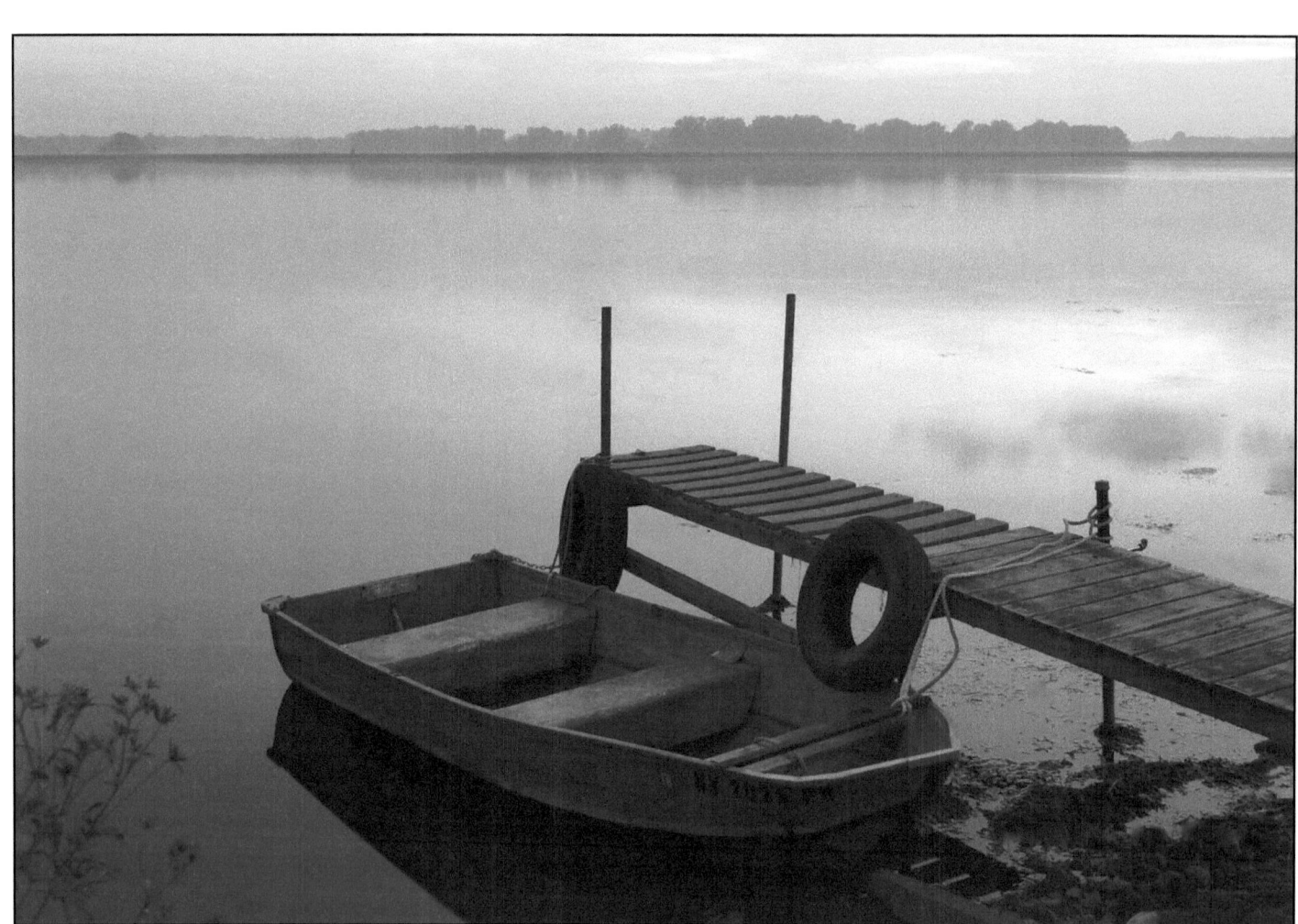

Tone

Dimension and texture
hold hands, one
imbedded in life,
the other smooth.

Leading and following
are not mutually exclusive.
season is motivation,
tone, the common bond.

It overcomes ripples
in life with mirrored heart.
I call it love. You call it
whatever you please.

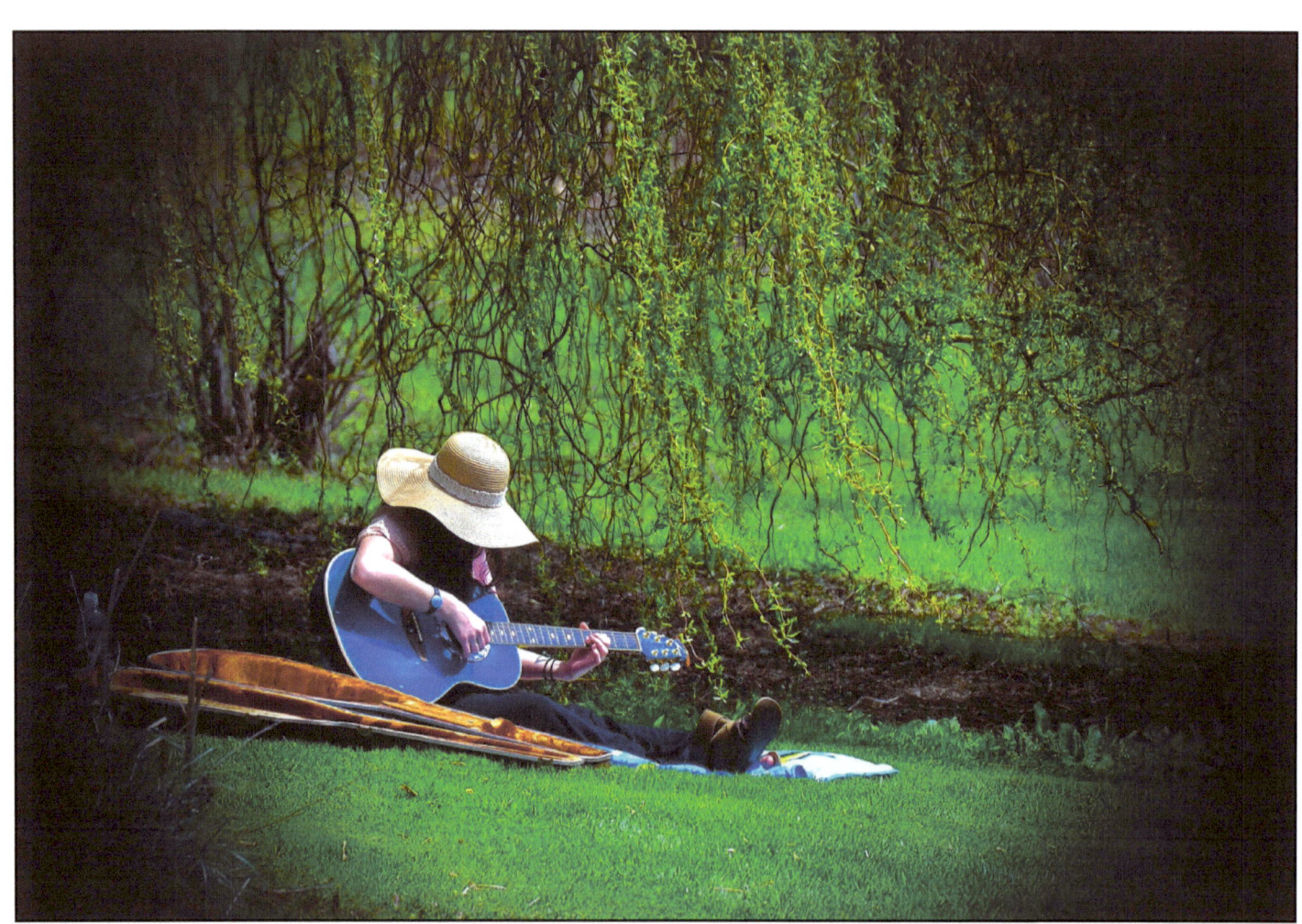

Sunlight writes the lyric
of nature's music.

The melody changes each time
we open our eyes.

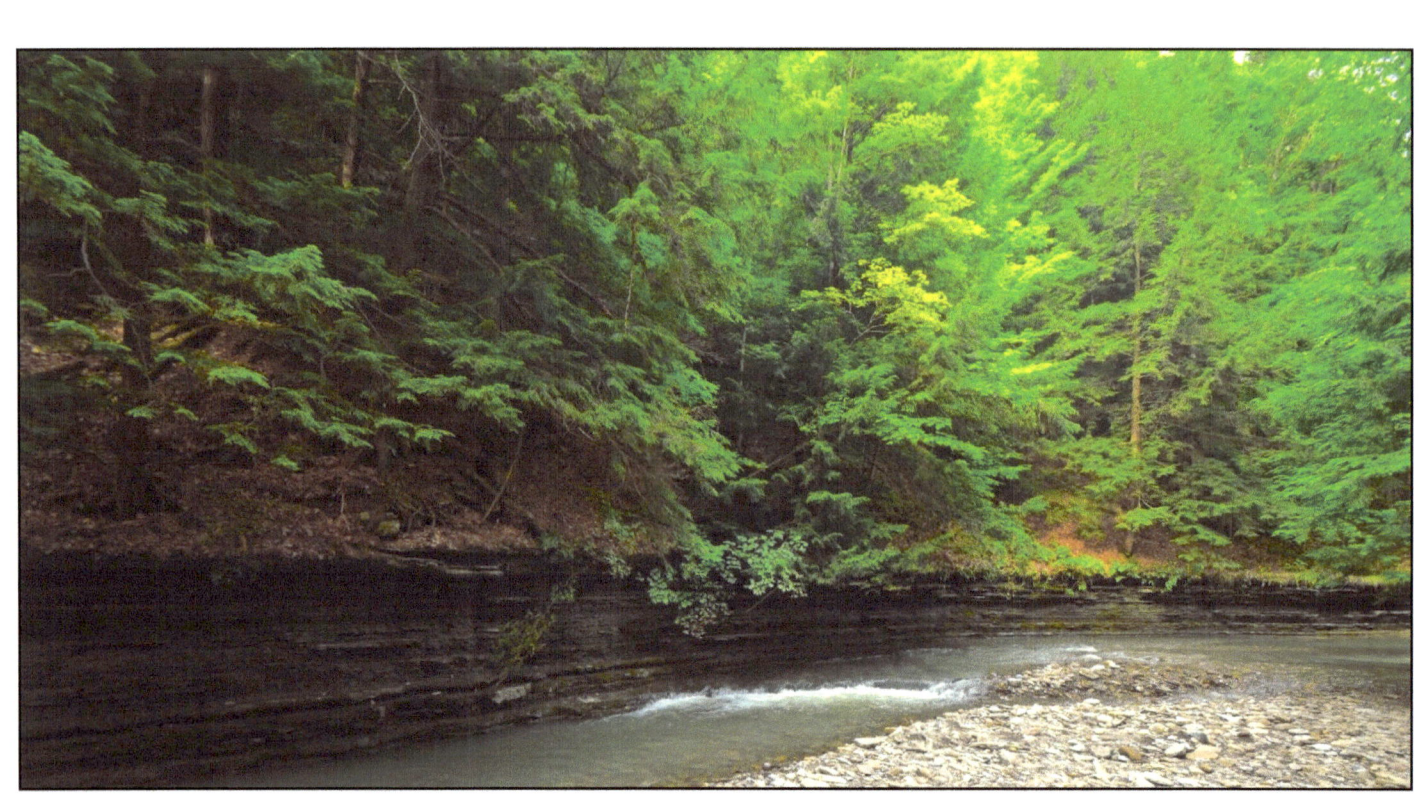

I drift as a breeze
over a forest, rest as
stones in the river.

A bird sings before
the moment ends.

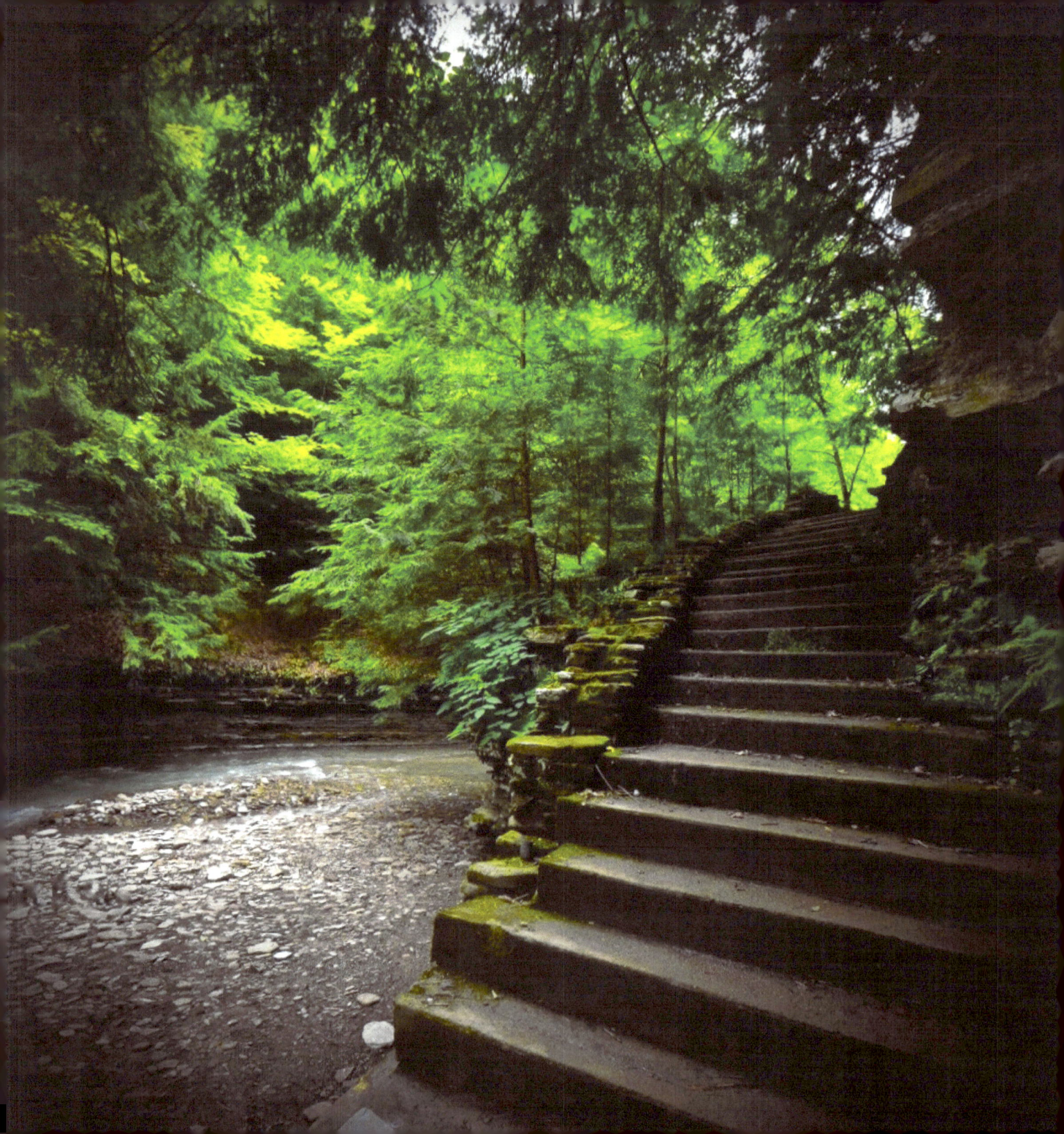

A creek flows to its logical destination,

our paths uncertain.

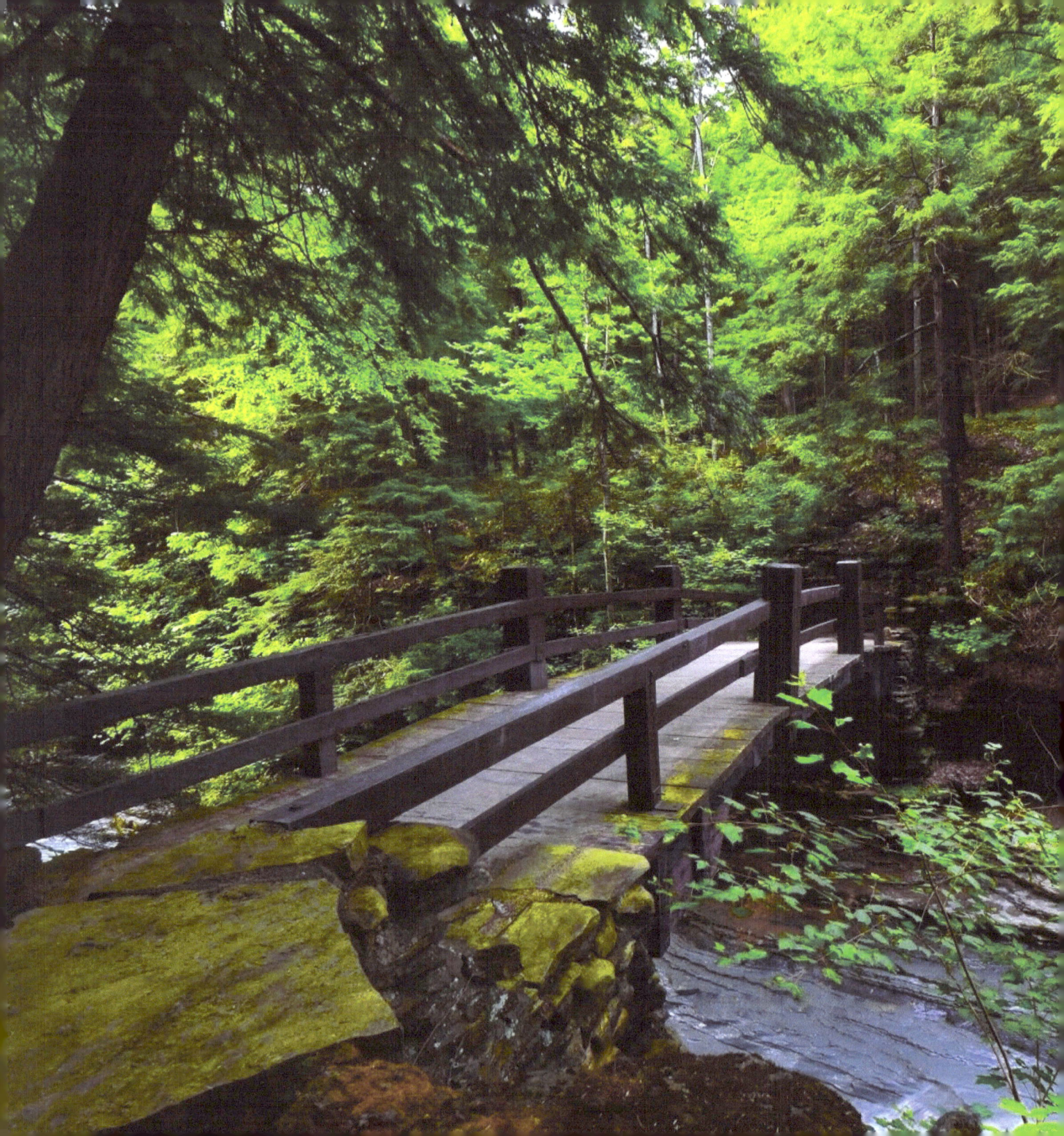

Both ends of a bridge look across to an unknown.

What we're crossing can be wondrous or daunting.

Midway, pause and breathe.

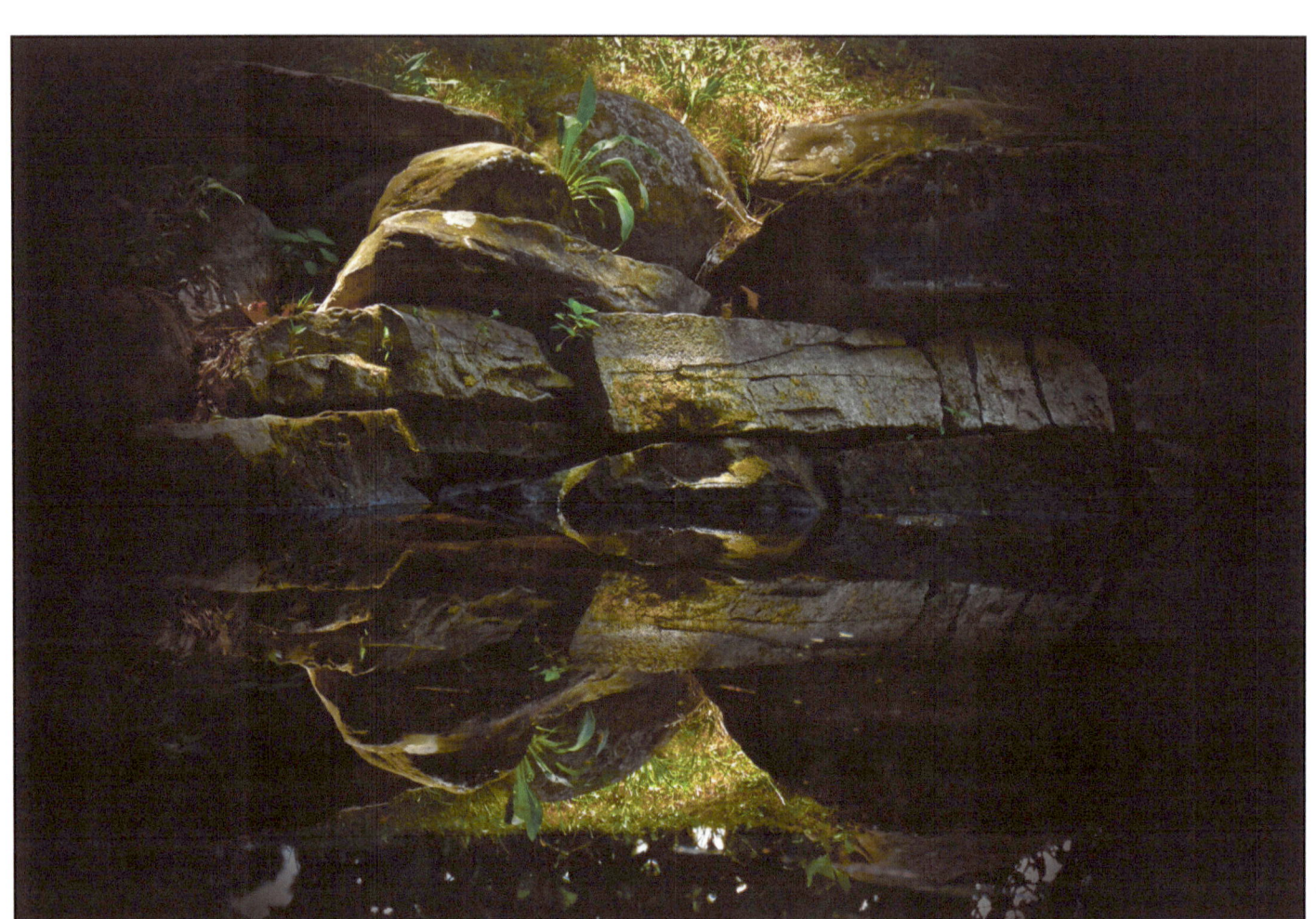

The earth is stone and water;

river and stream;

forest and plain.

I am reflection and calm,

this mid-year

moment.

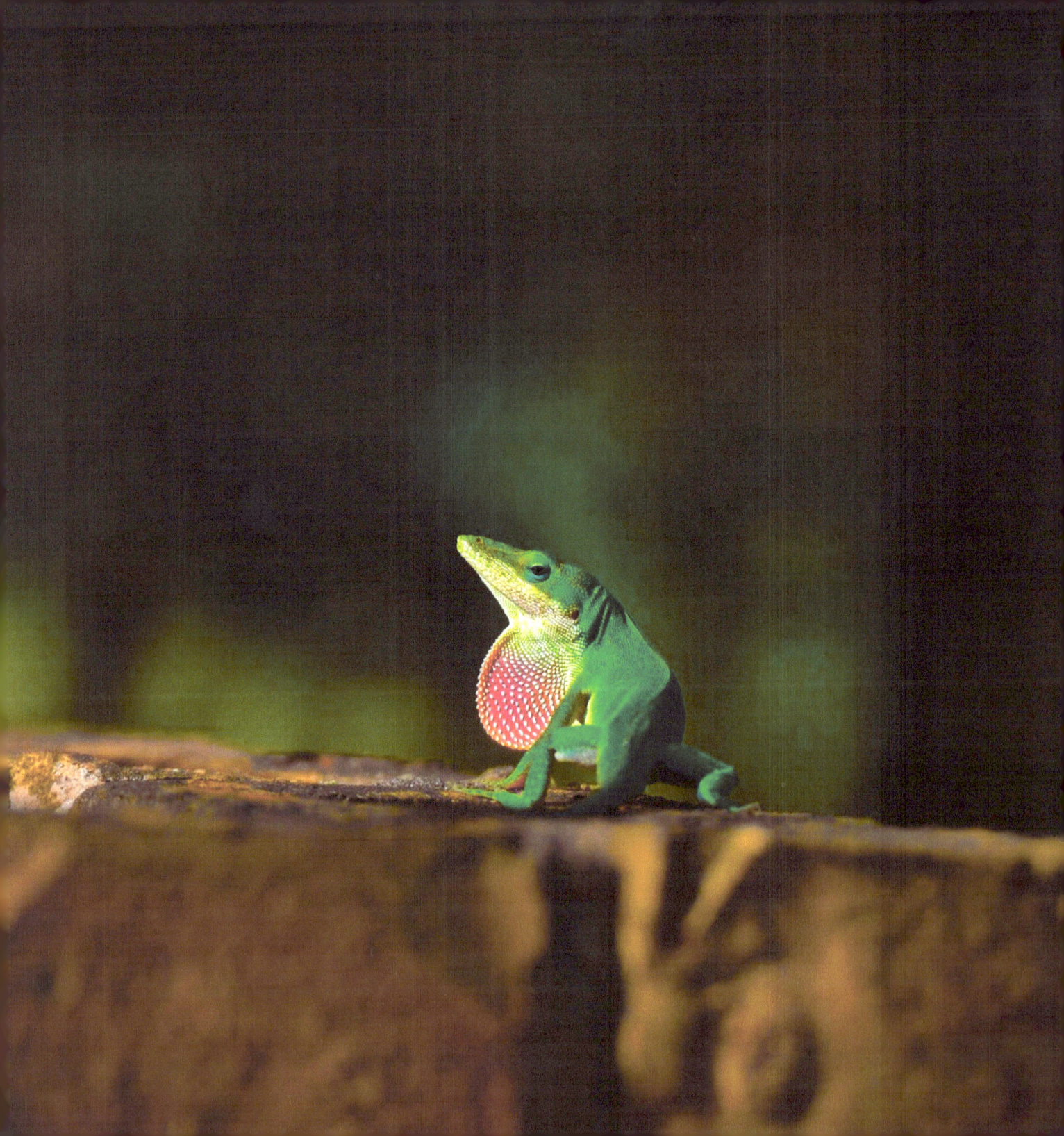

Deep in this season

I seek solitude,

and barter for

its moment.

Others do

as well.

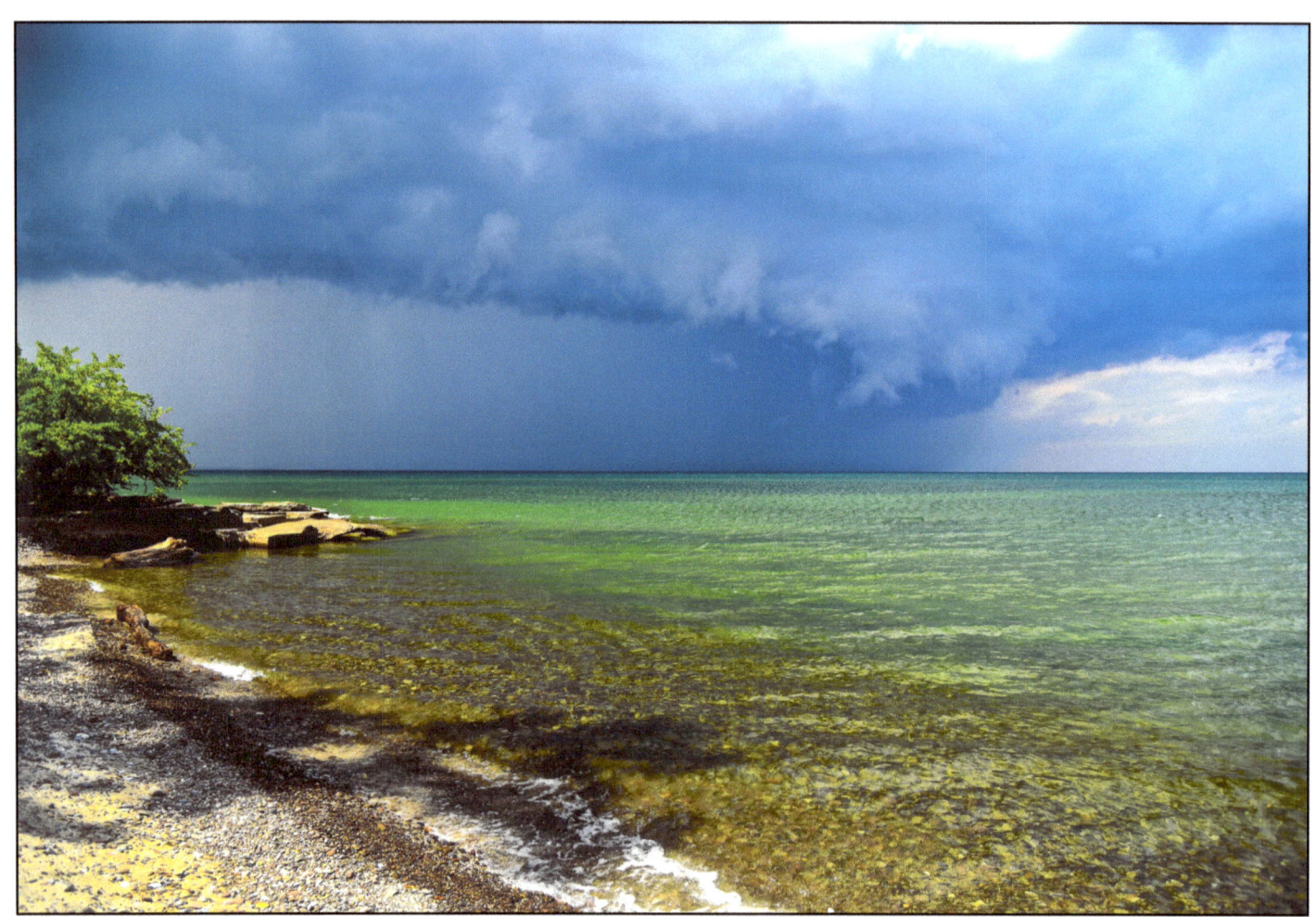

It's the

rain's

fragrance

we savor,

a break

in clouds

that makes

a storm

divine.

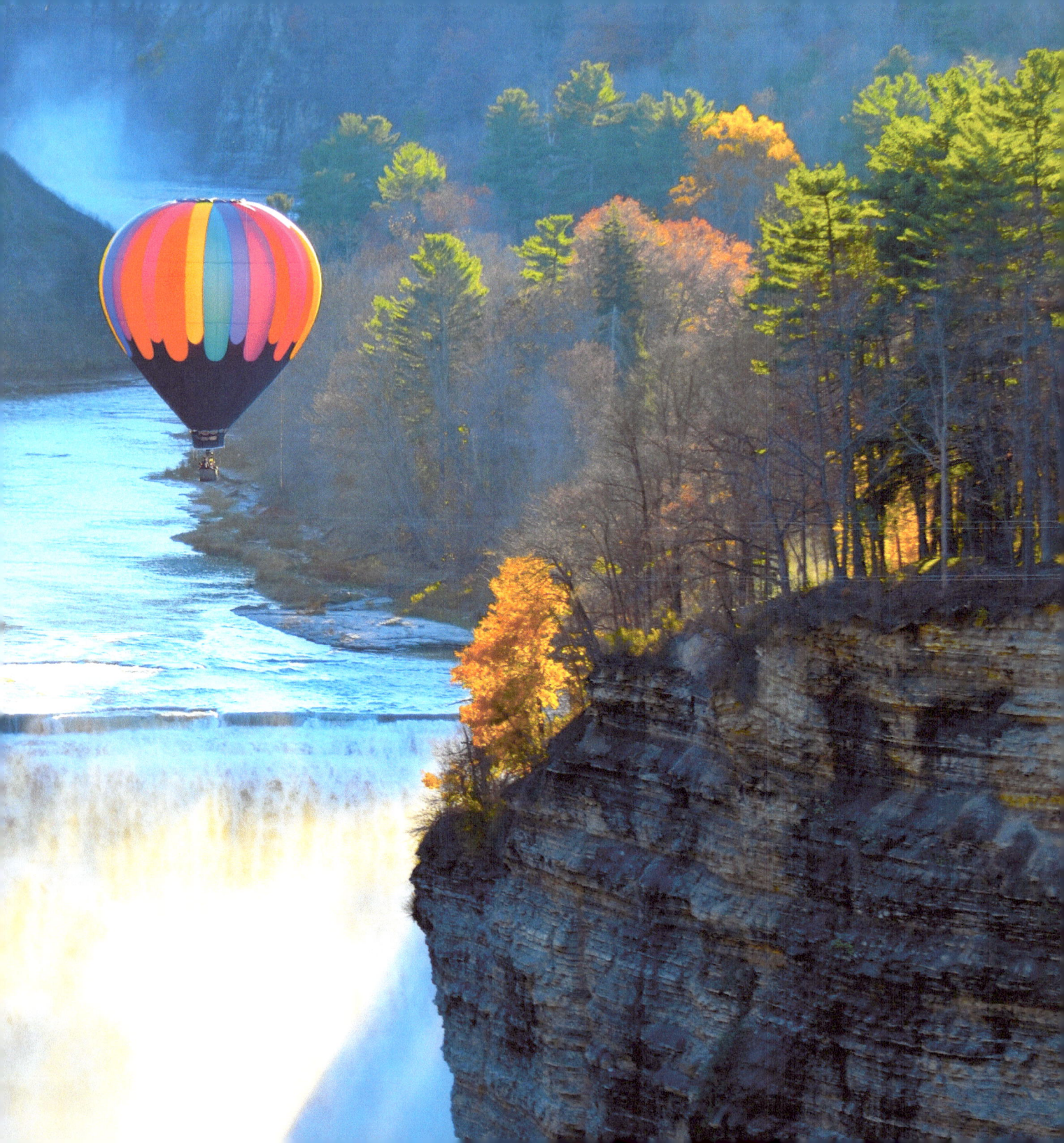

Rivers rise and fall,

twist and turn,

trickle and rage.

Strive for calm

above the chaos.

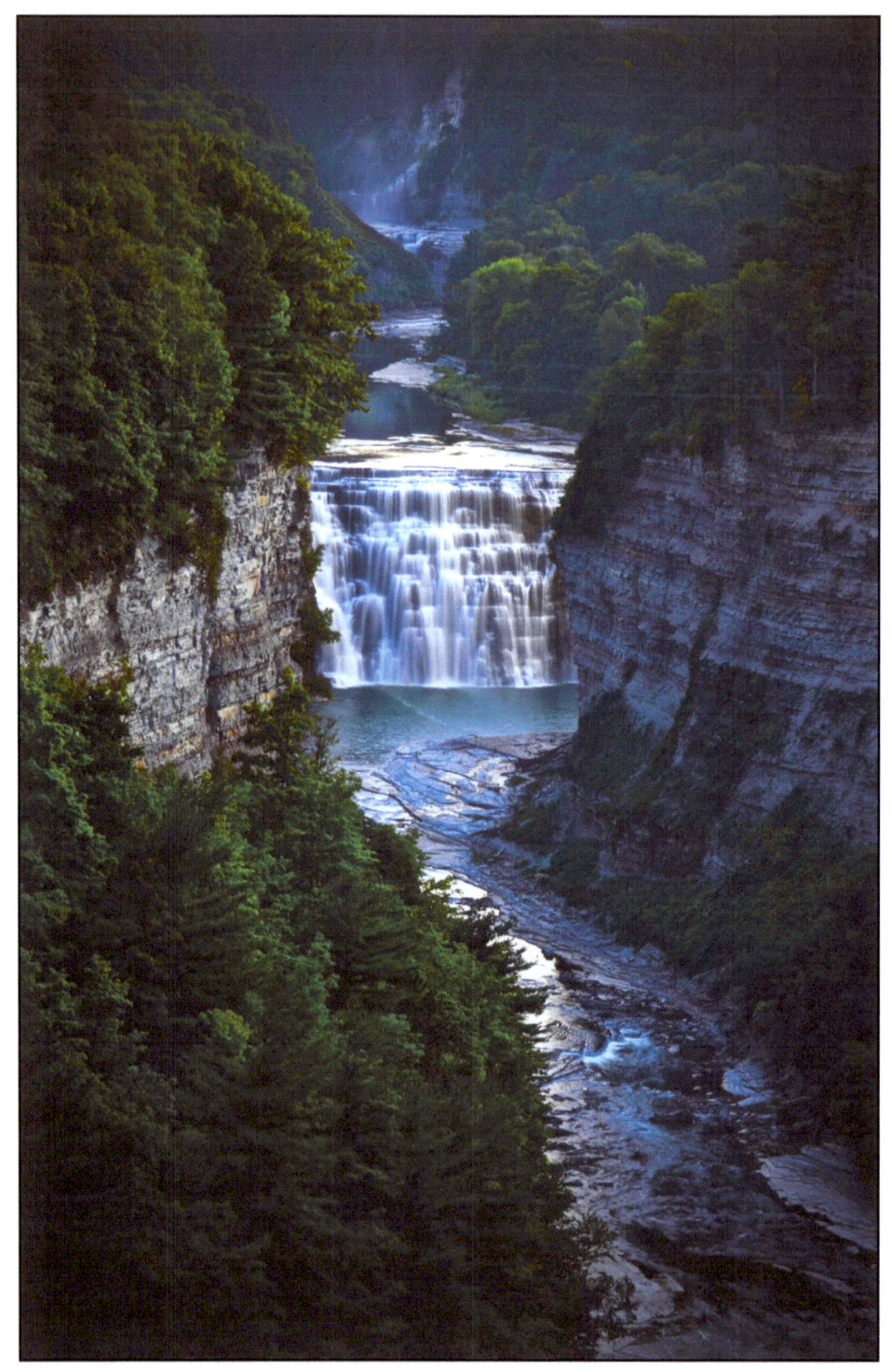

A river doesn't wait for seasons.
There is no past tense in a river.

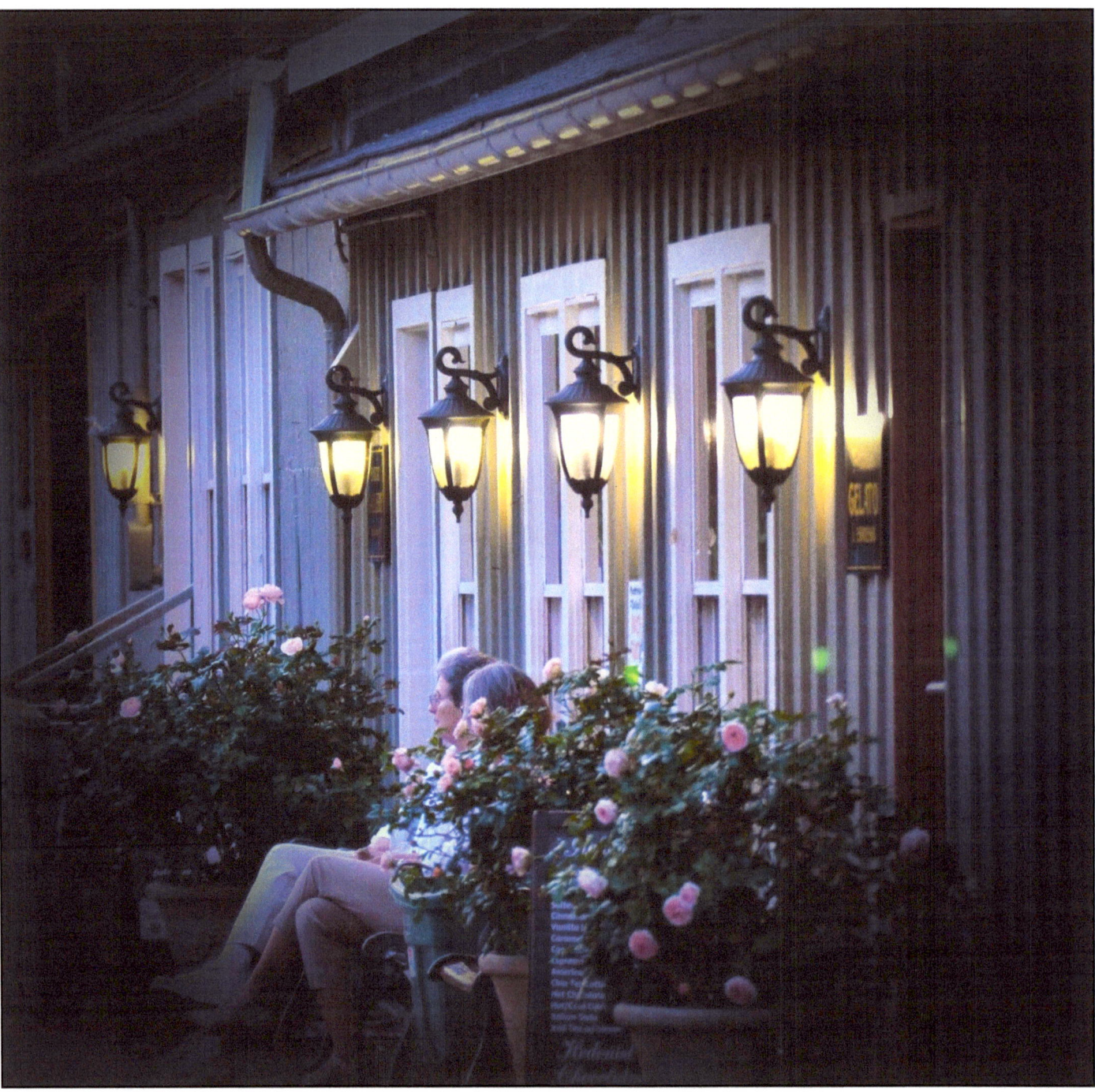

Evening measures distance
between memory and now.
Did you notice the color of
the rose's fading hue?

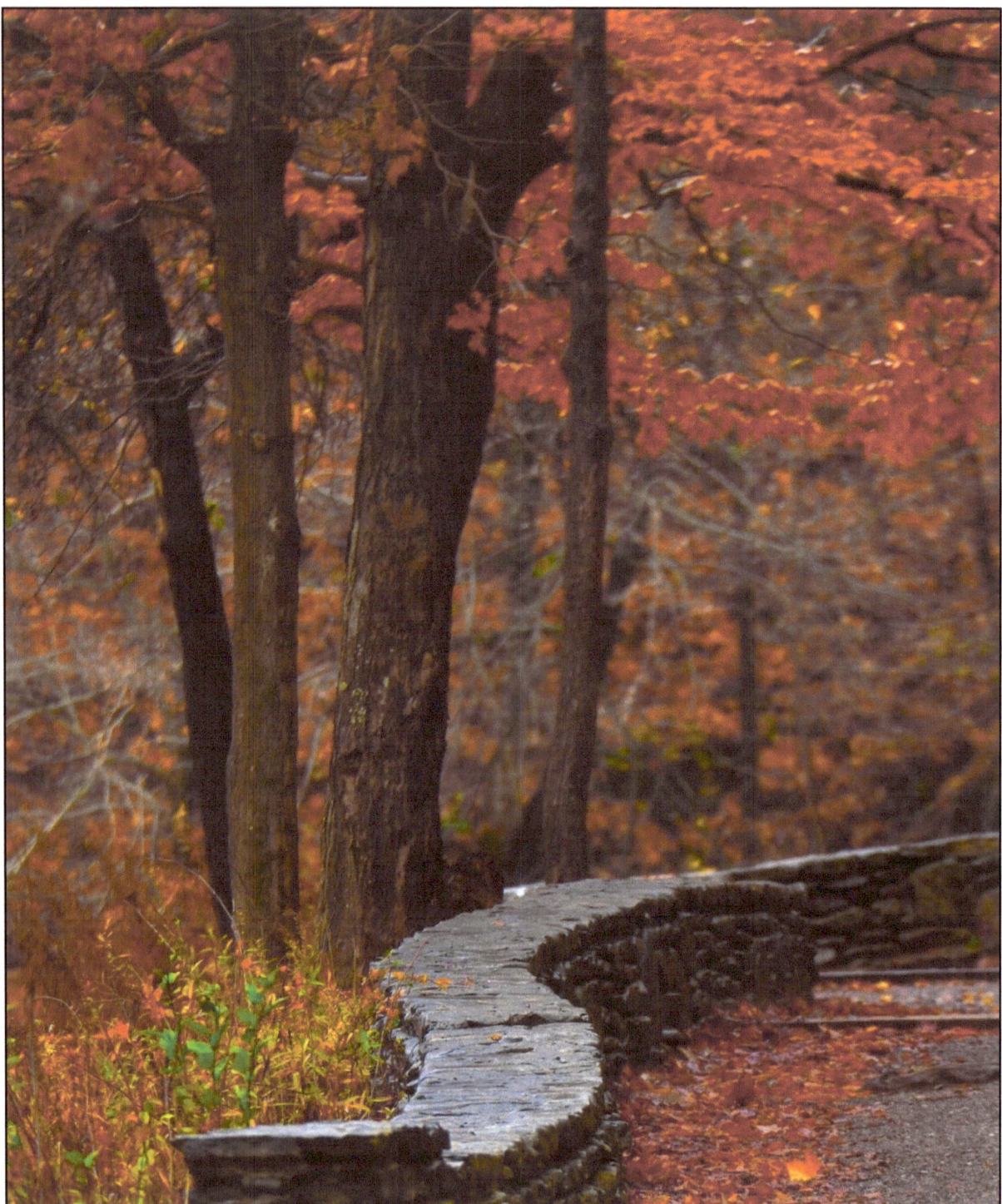

I look to the soul of a forest

as the great dying falls

crimson red around my feet.

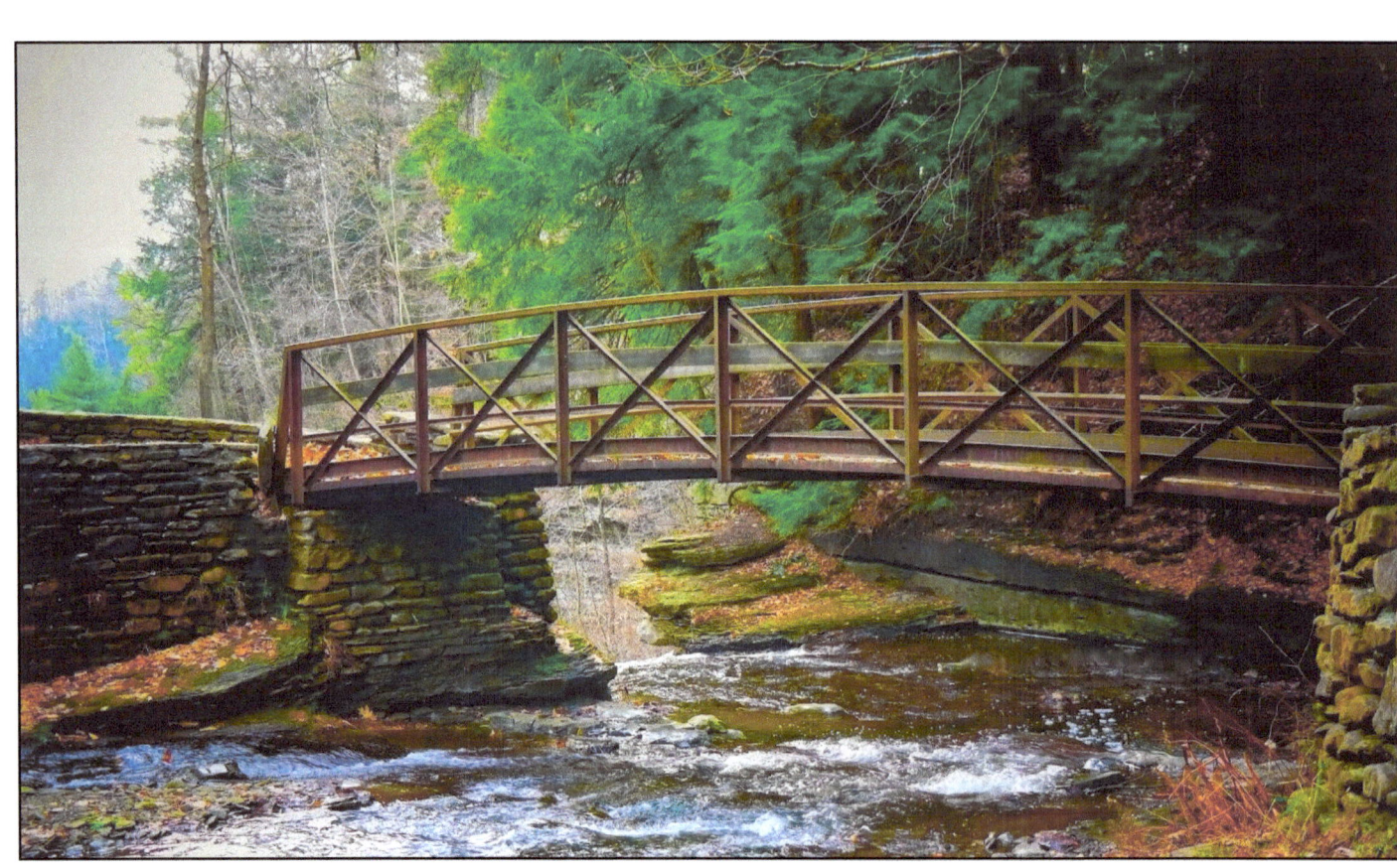

I carried you, you paused. I
held you, you moved unfazed.

Mid-autumn, let me be this one
season's pathway of steel and bone.

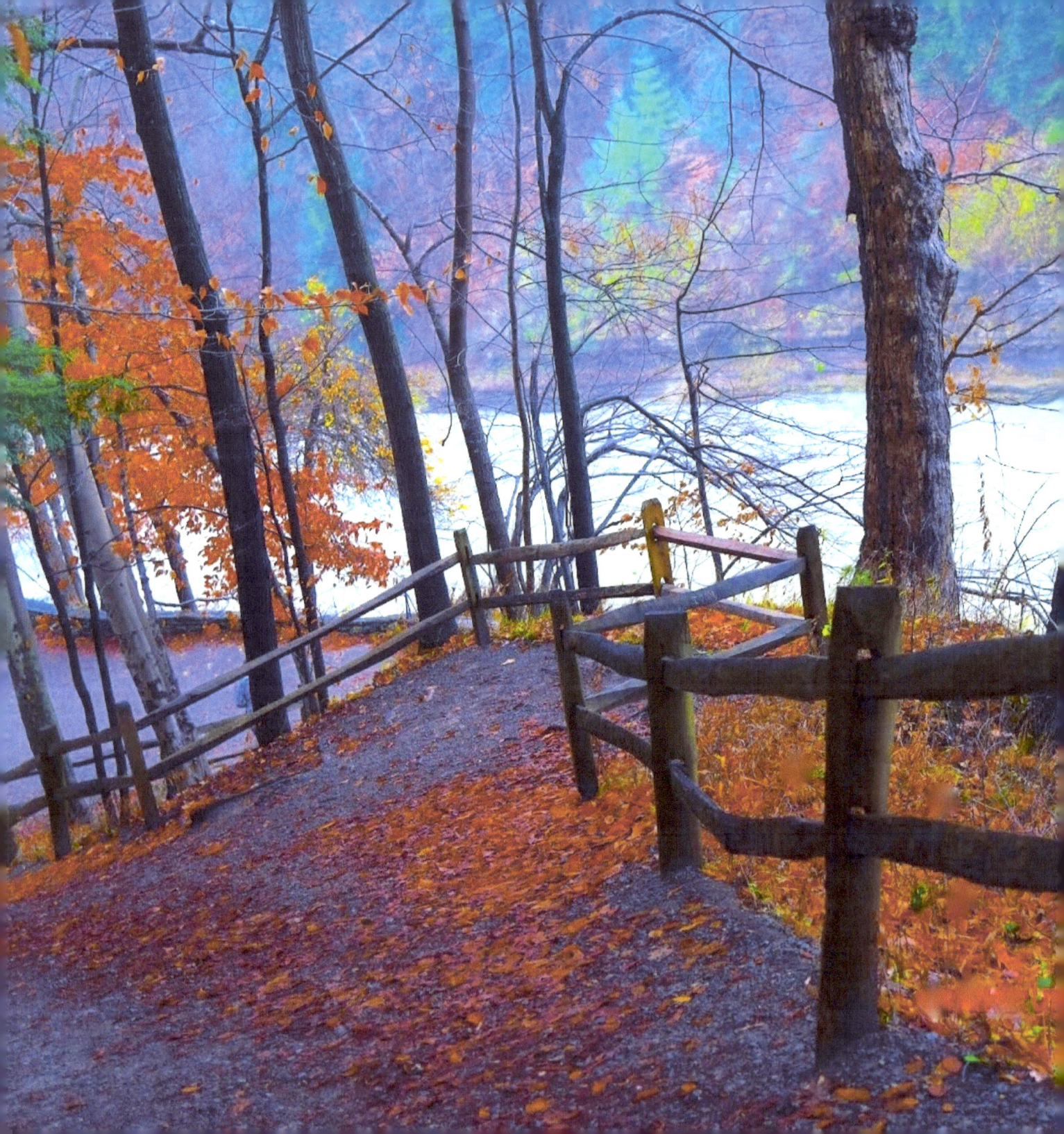

Beside this river-flow,
under November mist,
beneath fading hues,

seasons create paths.
We steady our eyes -
this downhill climb.

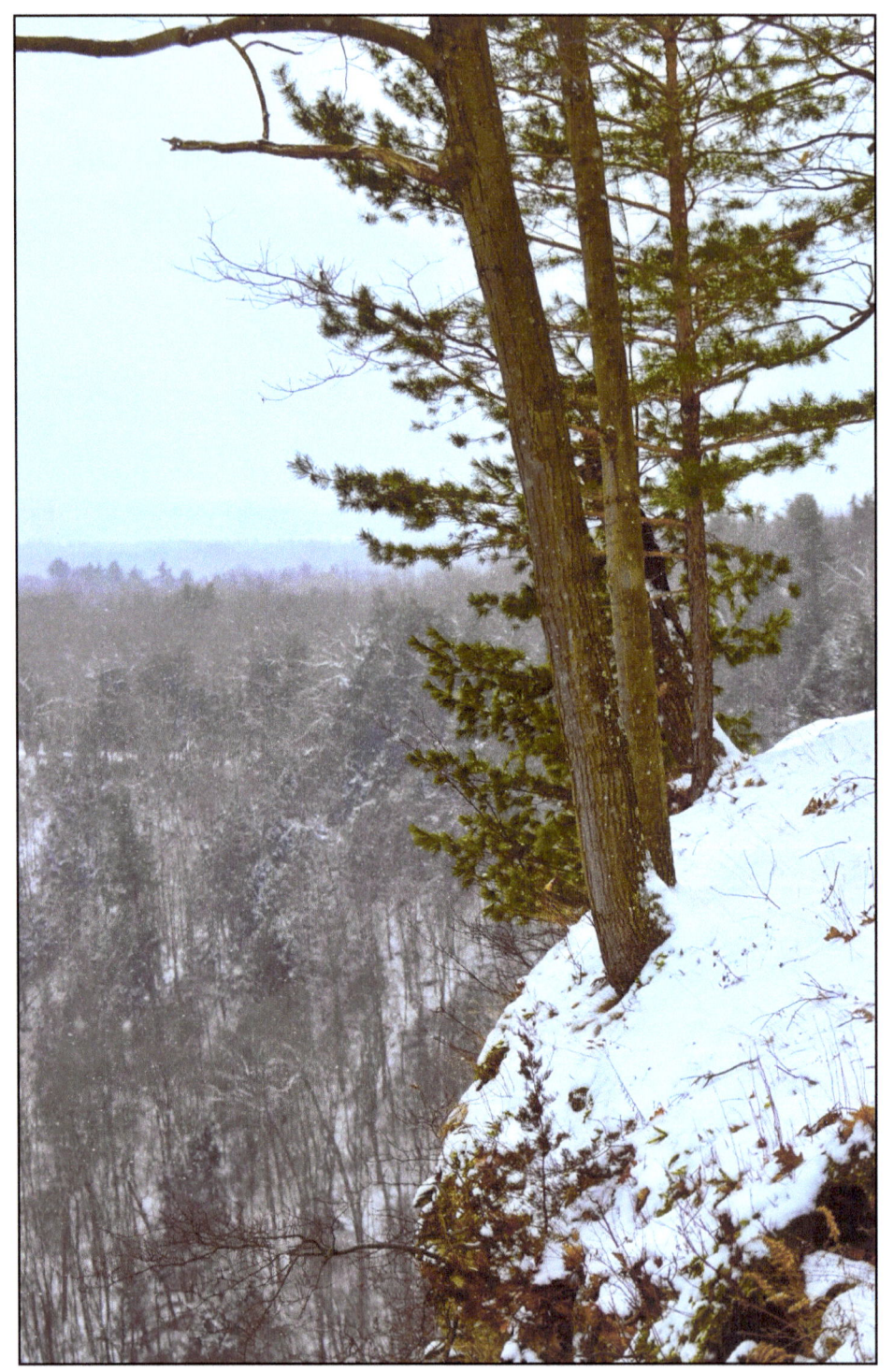

On the edge of seasons and Earth
trees turn toward Heaven.

There is no fear
in a tree.

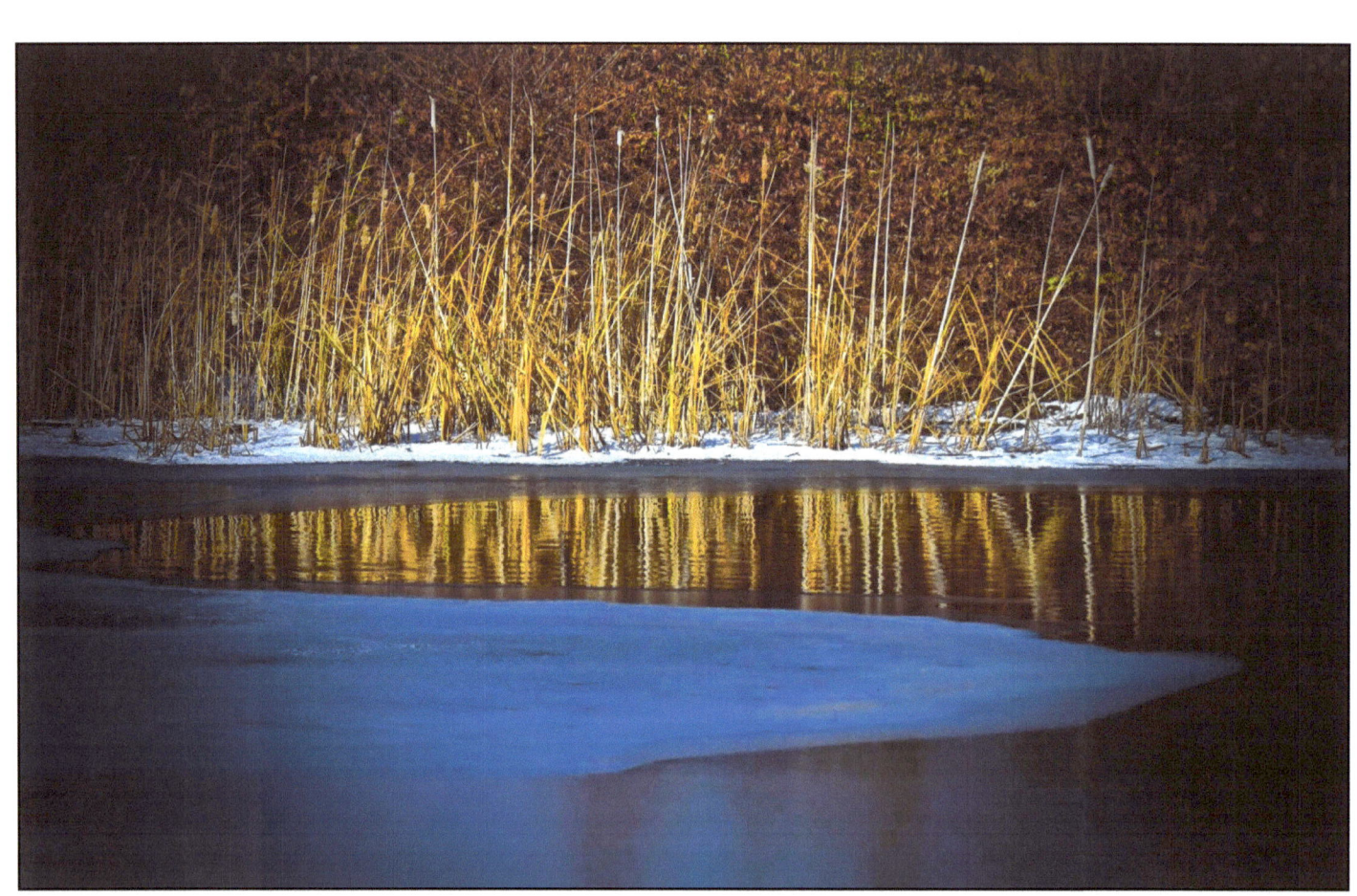

On the cusp of winter,
seasons compete for the pond.

Compromise is not an option.

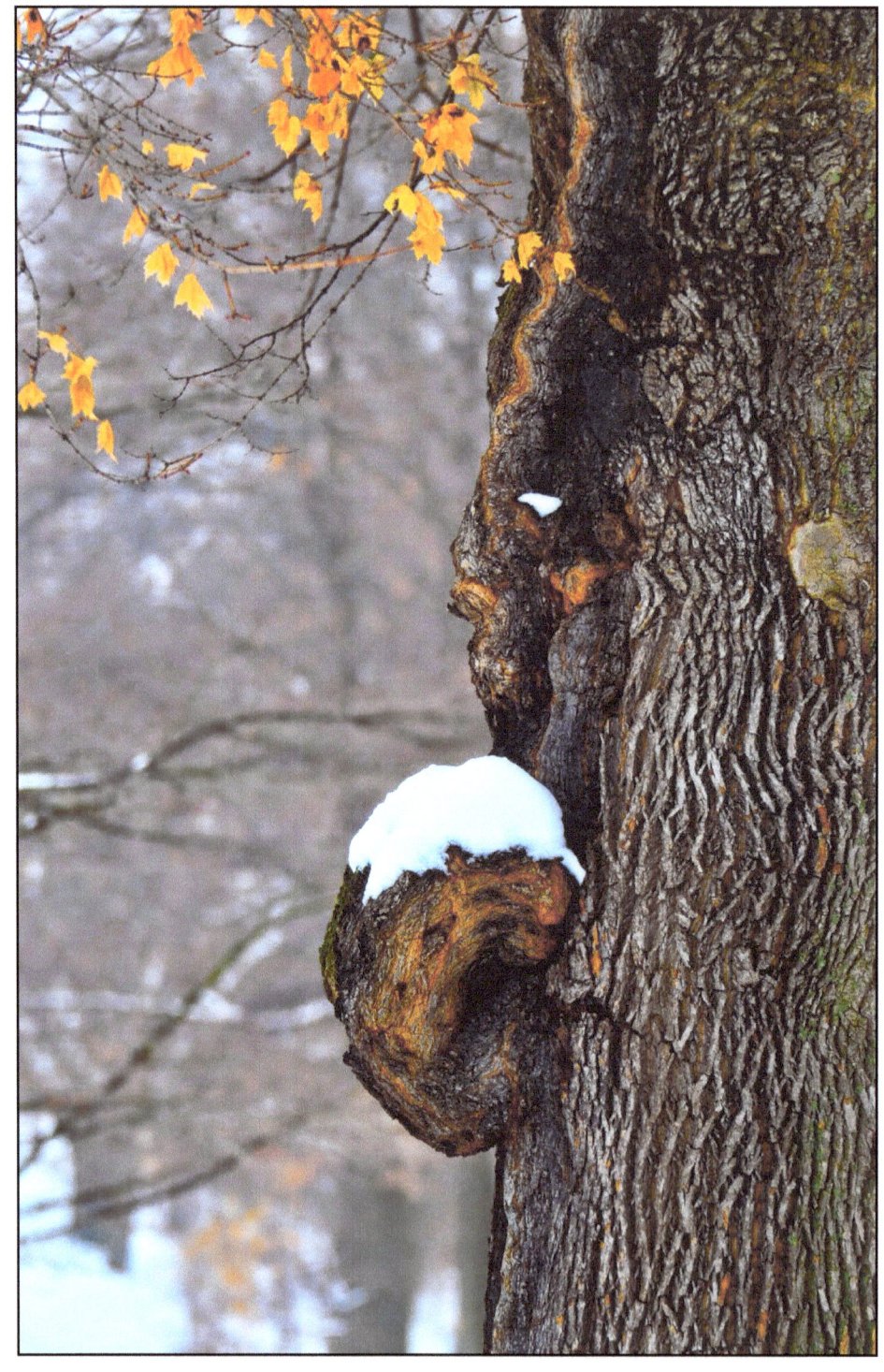

Seasons change.
Forests do, and endure.

We are forests.
Though we're changed
by the seasons,

we too, endure.

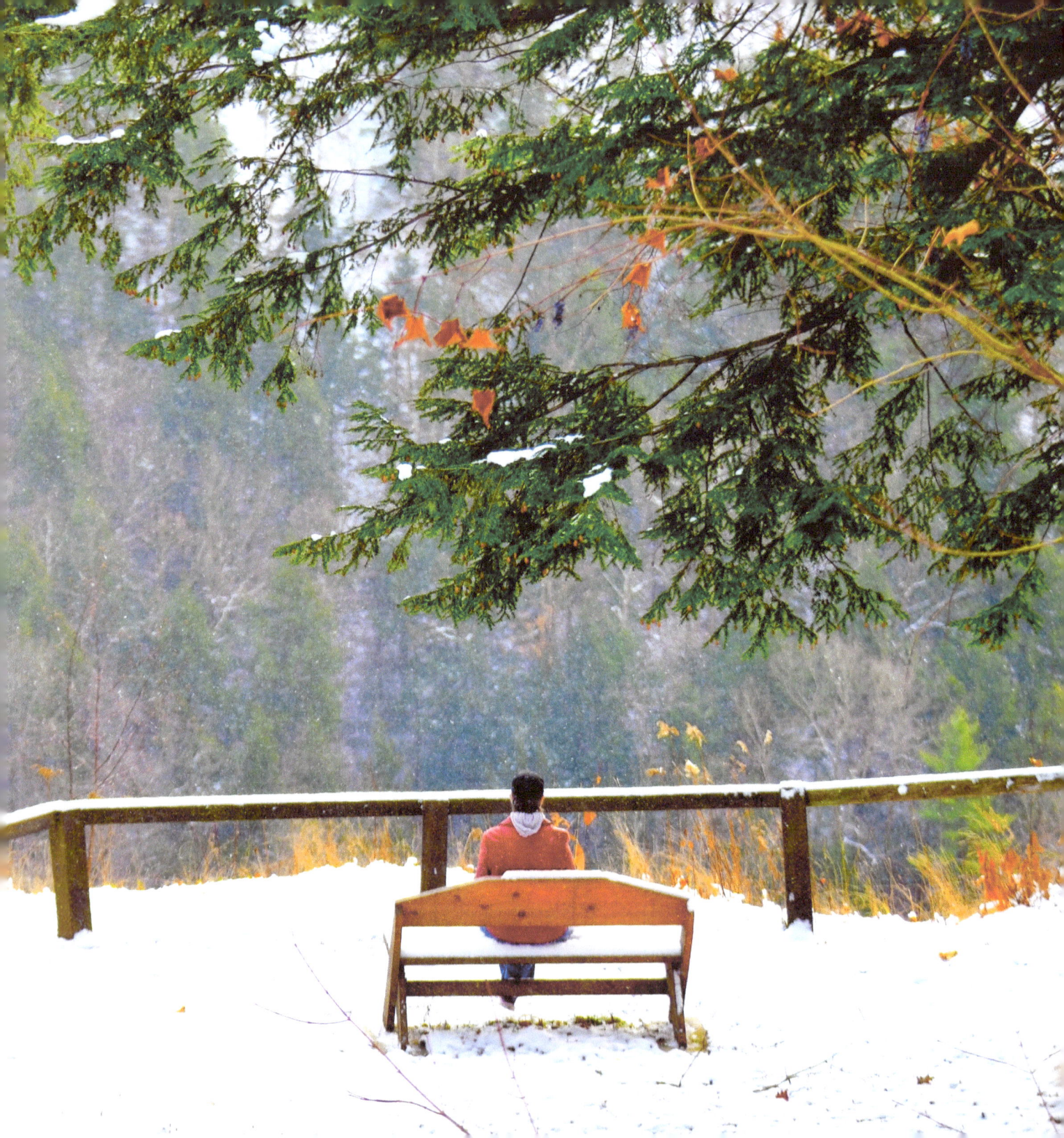

We humans create boundaries
to set limits.

Nature lives beyond
all that fakery.

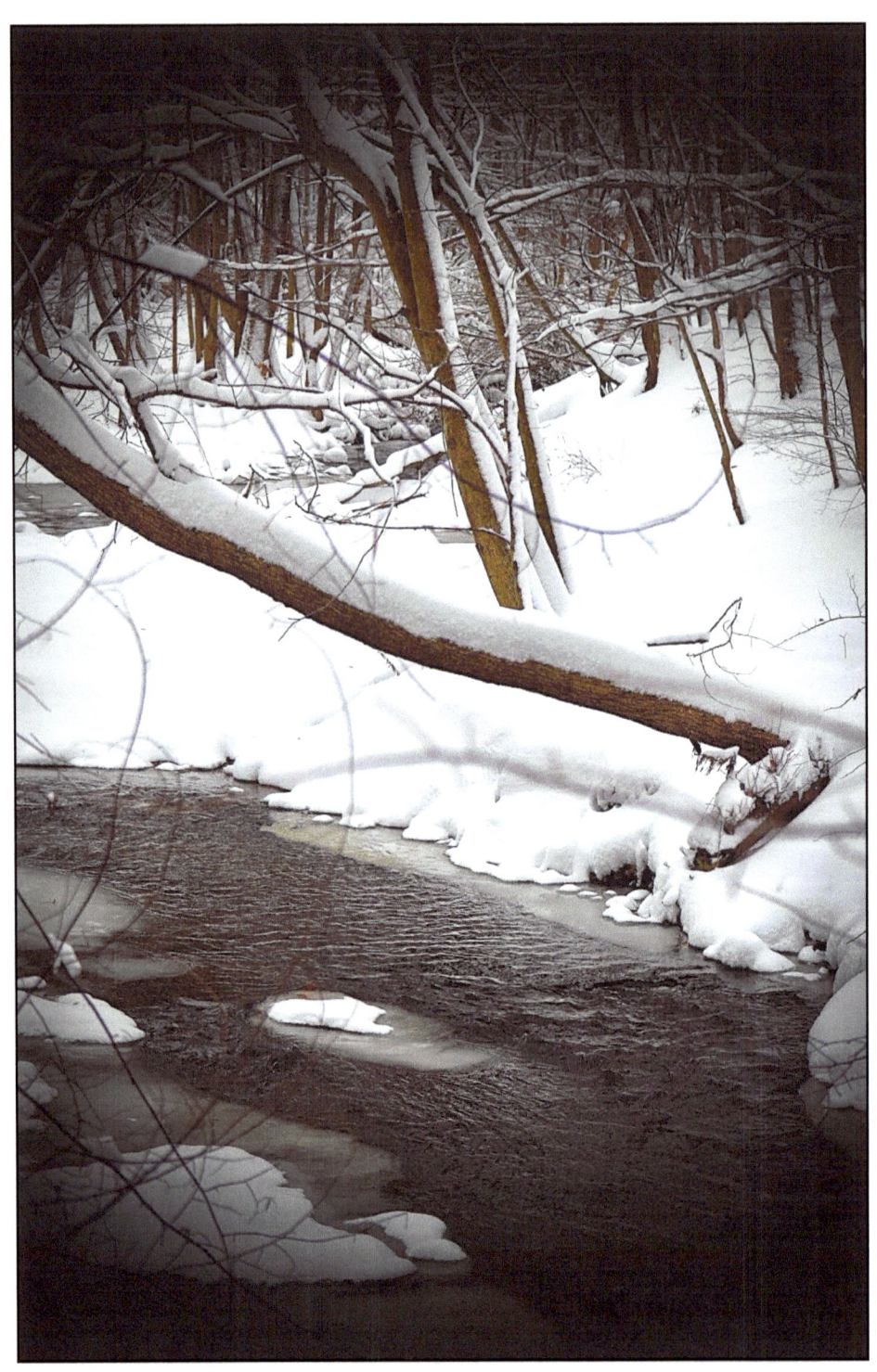

Winter is like lovers growing old.
Veins and bone emerge in proud
traditions of season. Foundations
of life are transparent. No secrets,
no pretense. No need to guide
the journey:

Listen to the
water as a stream becomes a river.

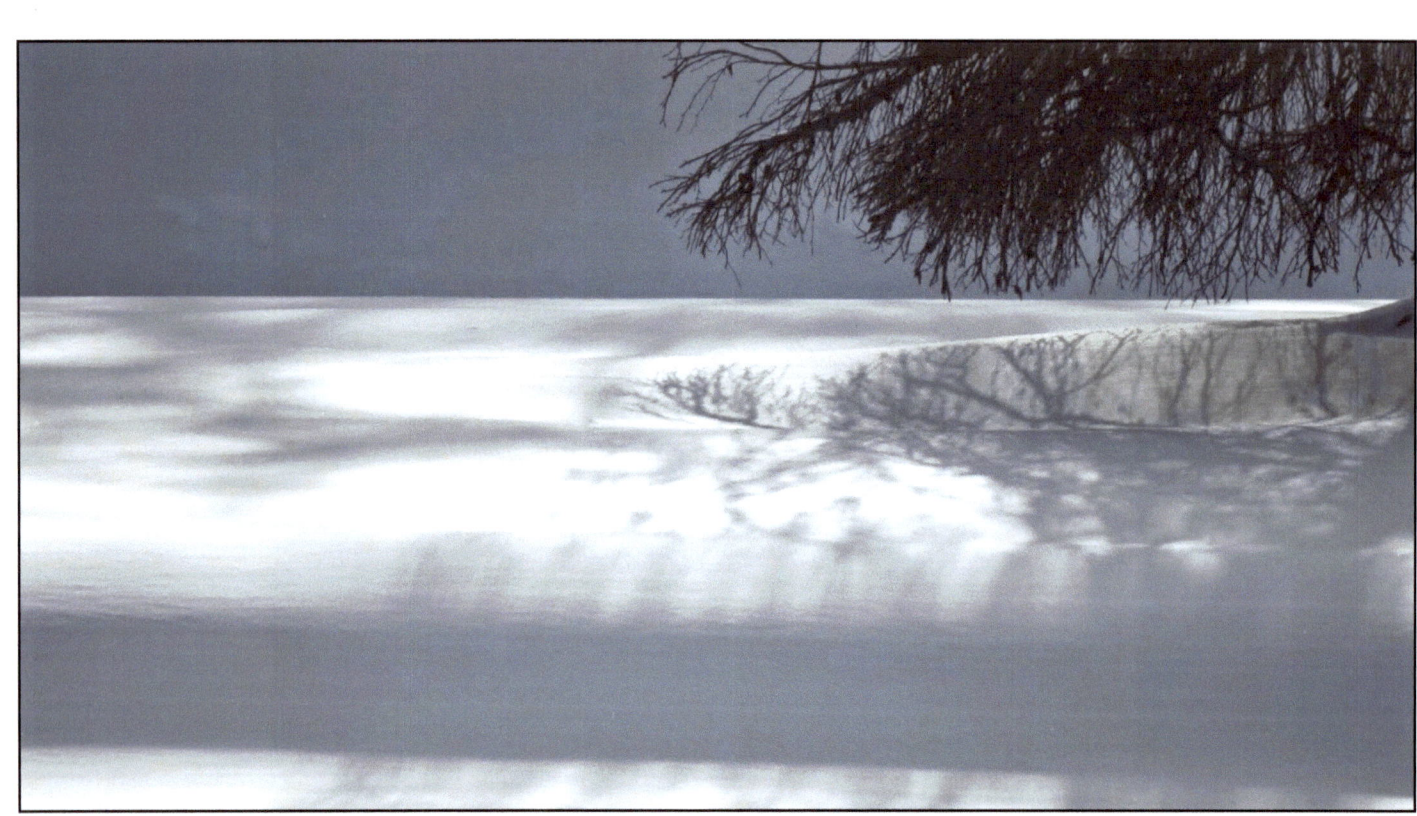

Sanctity is not only borne
on prayer, but manifest in rare
moments of visual perfection.

Even forests are reluctant to

cast shadows on new-fallen

snow.

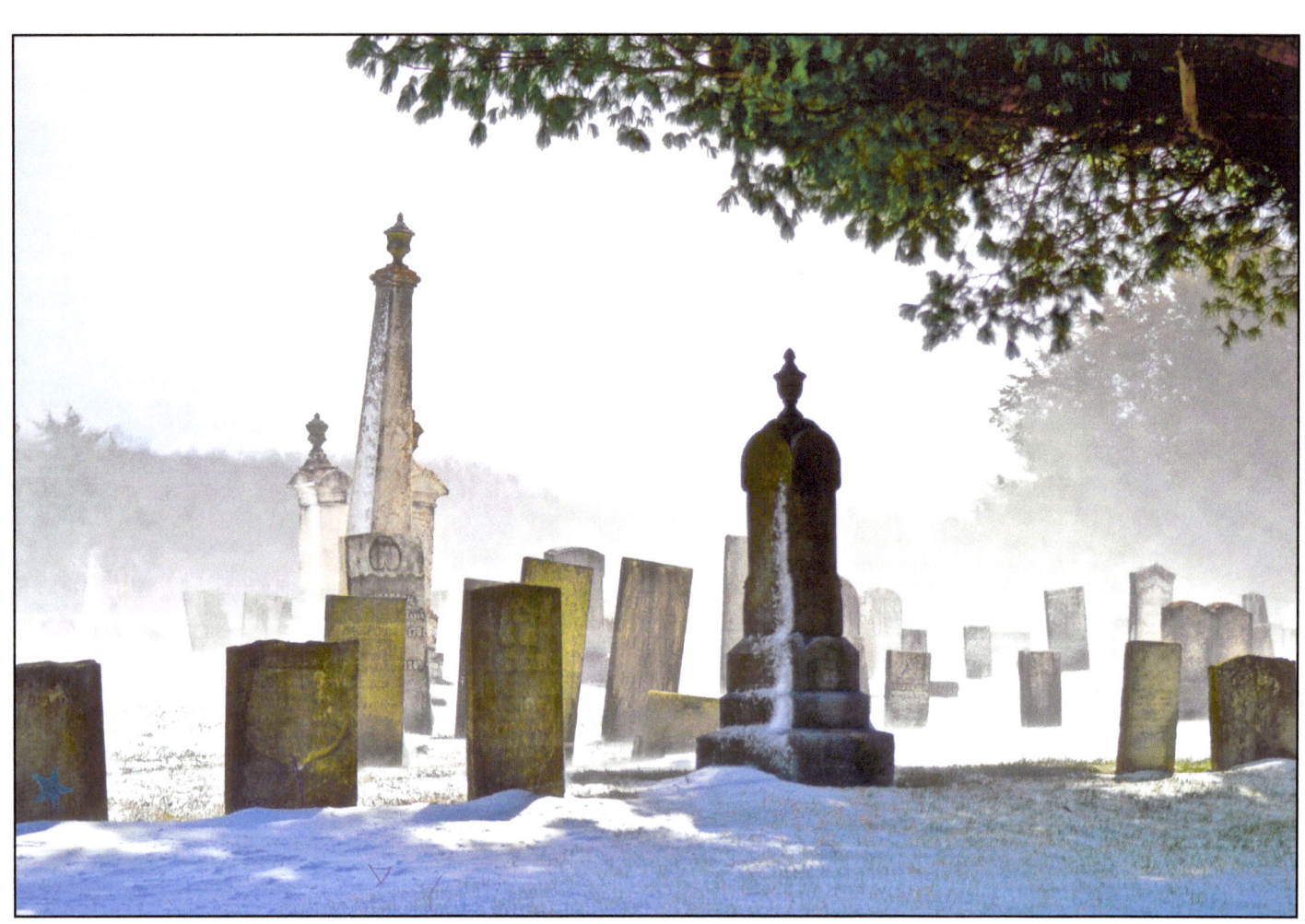

This temporal
portend to winter's
end is cause for
quiet elevation.

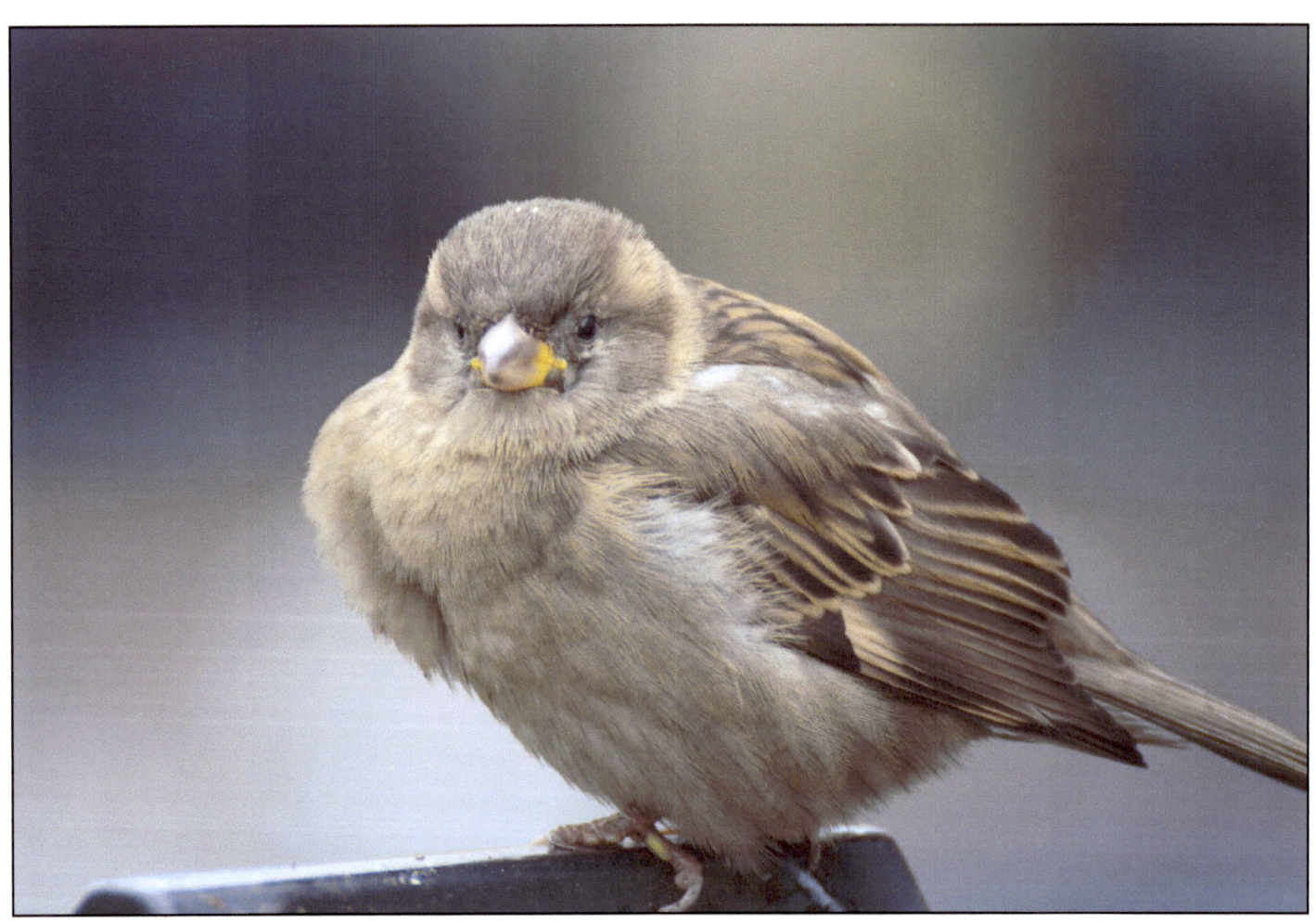

Bird can sing
through biting
winter wind;

Surely I can
breathe another
day till
spring.

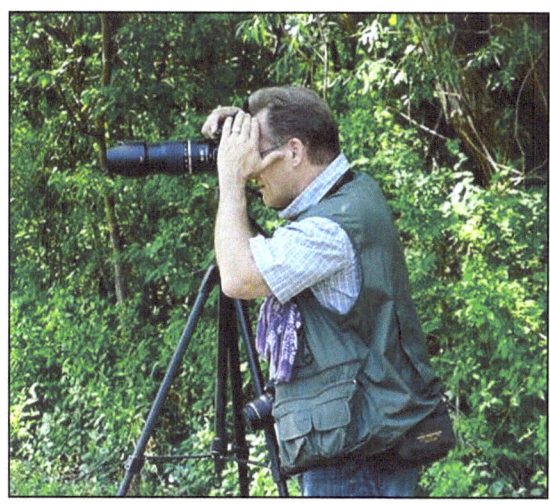

photo by: Pat Zarpentine

About the Author

Rick Burnett Baker, a native Texan, is a graduate of State University of New York (Albany) with a BA in Asian Studies, (minor in classical Chinese literature), a Graduate Certificate in US Urban Policy, and a Masters (MRP) in Regional and Urban Planning, Third World. After several months in the early 70's with a mining company in Honduras he worked for three years in Saudi Arabia with a civil engineering firm from Houston, and worked throughout Southeast Asia, China, and Northern Africa with Halliburton for nearly a decade, based out of Singapore. During his years living in Singapore he was also known for his radio and television voice-over work. Baker returned to the US in 1985 to complete academic interests and continues to live in New York.

Photo Index

www.ingramcontent.com/pod-product-compliance
Lightning Source LLC
Chambersburg PA
CBHW050747180526
45159CB00003B/1379